An Illustrated History of
Islamic Art & Design

An Illustrated History of
Islamic Art & Design

AN INTRODUCTION TO THE ART OF ISLAM, INCLUDING CALLIGRAPHY, TILES, CERAMICS, GLASS, STONE, CARVINGS, METALWORK, COSTUME AND CARPETS

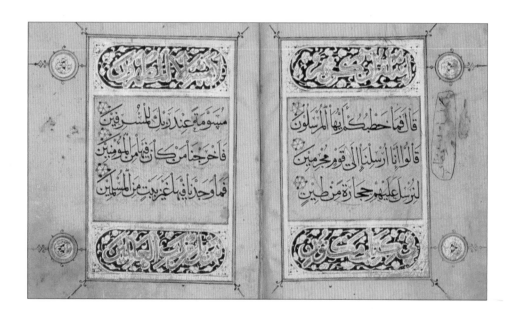

SHOWN IN OVER 240 PHOTOGRAPHS OF PAINTINGS, ORNAMENTS AND TEXTILES

CONSULTANT: MOYA CAREY

CAROLINE CHAPMAN • MELANIE GIBSON •
GEORGE MANGINIS • ANNA McSWEENEY •
CHARLES PHILLIPS • IAIN ZACZEK

southwater

This edition is published by Southwater
an imprint of Anness Publishing Ltd
Blaby Road, Wigston
Leicestershire LE18 4SE
info@anness.com
www.southwaterbooks.com; www.annesspublishing.com

Anness Publishing has a new picture agency outlet for images
for publishing, promotions or advertising. Please visit our website
www.practicalpictures.com for more information.

Publisher: Joanna Lorenz
Editorial Director: Helen Sudell
Cover Design: Oil Often
Production Controller: Christine Ni

Produced for Anness Publishing by Toucan Books
Managing Editor: Ellen Dupont
Editor: Theresa Bebbington
Designer: Ralph Pitchford
Picture Researcher: Marian Pullen
Cartography: Cosmographics, UK
Proofreader: Marion Dent
Indexer: Michael Dent

ETHICAL TRADING POLICY
At Anness Publishing we believe that business should be conducted in an
ethical and ecologically sustainable way, with respect for the environment
and a proper regard to the replacement of the natural resources we employ.

As a publisher, we use a lot of wood pulp in high-quality paper for
printing, and that wood commonly comes from spruce trees. We are
therefore currently growing more than 750,000 trees in three Scottish
forest plantations: Berrymoss (130 hectares/320 acres), West Touxhill
(125 hectares/305 acres) and Deveron Forest (75 hectares/185 acres).
The forests we manage contain more than 3.5 times the number of trees
employed each year in making paper for the books we manufacture.

Because of this ongoing ecological investment programme, you, as our
customer, can have the pleasure and reassurance of knowing that a tree is
being cultivated on your behalf to naturally replace the materials used to
make the book you are holding.

Our forestry programme is run in accordance with the UK Woodland
Assurance Scheme (UKWAS) and will be certified by the internationally
recognized Forest Stewardship Council (FSC). The FSC is a non-
government organization dedicated to promoting responsible management
of the world's forests. Certification ensures forests are managed in an
environmentally sustainable and socially responsible way. For further
information about this scheme, go to www.annesspublishing.com/trees.

Previously published as part of a larger volume,
The Illustrated Encyclopedia of Islamic Art and Architecture

PUBLISHER'S NOTE
Although the information in this book is believed to be accurate and
true at the time of going to press, neither the authors nor the publisher
can accept any legal responsibility or liability for any errors or omissions
that may have been made.

Page 2 Illustration of Adam and Eve (c.1550) from the
Falnama, *attributed to the sixth Shiah Imam, Jafar al-Sadiq.*
Page 3 Calligraphy from a 14th-century Quran.

CONTENTS

*Above Early Qurans were written on horizontal leaves of
parchment. The* kufic *script has long, horizontal strokes.*

Above 19th-century Iranian tiles depicting two noblemen hunting, one with a falcon, the other with a bow and arrow.

Above This 17th-century Star Ushak rug uses quatrefoil (four-leaved) medallions with smaller diamonds.

INTRODUCTION

Western art historians have long used the expression Islamic Art to describe the wide range of visual culture that has been created in the extensive regions of the world – from Spain to India, Turkey to North Africa – that have at some time come under Muslim rule. The glorious arts of the book, such as calligraphy, painting, manuscript illumination and bookbinding, not to mention luxury items made from precious metals and alloys, ivory, rock crystal, gemstones, glass, ceramics and wood, and textiles and carpets, all qualify as Islamic Art.

Their splendid refinement signifies a longstanding culture of taste and discernment and an educated, perhaps elite, audience. The common factor in this great output from so many different cultures is the religion of Islam, for although the civilian populations of Western Asia and other parts of the Islamic world were never exclusively Muslim, they have long been ruled by caliphs, sultans, shahs and amirs who were.

The Islamic world has created an incredible wealth of art treasures. The 8th to 10th centuries are renowned as a golden age for Islamic culture where luxury arts thrived: metalworkers, weavers and potters produced beautiful, highly crafted objects, while scribes created the first Qurans to be produced on paper. In the 10th century, Fatimid art was influenced by the late-antique figurative traditions of the classical world. Written accounts from the Fatimid era describe incredible levels of luxury and sophistication, while exquisite objects made from carved wood, ivory and rock crystal and lustreware were also produced for the cosmopolitan merchant elite.

In India, the three greatest Mughal emperors, Akbar (reigned 1556–1605), Jahangir (reigned 1605–27) and Shah Jahan (reigned 1628–58), presided over a period of enormous wealth and power, with great creativity and exuberance in art, reaching unprecedented opulence in decorative objects, paintings, jewellery and carpets.

This beautifully illustrated book explores this wonderful and rich heritage, from the first caliphal dynasty of the Islamic empire founded by al-Muawiyah of the Umayyad clan in 661 to the art of 19th-century Iran.

Divided into three sections, the first one, Manuscripts and Paintings, embraces the Holy Quran and describes how it has been a focus for Islamic art across the centuries, as well as looking at the art of luxury manuscripts and great paintings. This is followed by Pottery, Glass, Tiles and Stone, which features a range of beautiful Islamic ornaments, from geometric patterns that decorate ceramics and the different techniques for cutting and colouring glassware to detailed carved stone. The final section, Carvings, Metalwork, Costume and Carpets describes how the skilled artisans throughout the centuries created superb pieces from prized materials such as rock crystal, jade, ivory and precious metals as well as fine and luxurious carpets.

Meticulously researched, and lavishly illustrated with more than 240 photographs, reproductions and paintings, this superb book offers a wonderful overview of the rich heritage of Islamic art.

Left A Shahnama *scene attributed to Sultan Muhammad shows the hero Faridun striking the tyrant Zahhak with an ox-head mace.*

Opposite *This exquisite millennial rock crystal mug dates from around 975.*

TIMELINE

THE FOLLOWING TIMELINE LISTS SOME OF THE MAJOR WORKS IN THE LONG HISTORY OF ISLAMIC ART AND ARCHITECTURE.

- 610–32 The Prophet receives the revelations of the Quran.
- *c.*654 A standardized version of the Quran is issued by Rashidun Caliph Uthman ibn-Affan (reigned 644–56) and sent to the four cities of Madinah, Damascus, Kufa and Basra.
- 691 Umayyad Caliph Abd al-Malik (reigned 685–705) oversees the building of the Dome of the Rock in Jerusalem.
- 696–98 A major reform of coinage in the Umayyad Caliphate replaces figurative images with Islamic epigraphy.
- 705–15 The Great Mosque in Damascus is built under Umayyad Caliph al-Walid I (reigned 705–15). It is one of the first mosques to have minarets.
- *c.* 712–715 The Qusayr Amra 'desert palace', or hunting lodge, is built by Caliph al-Walid I in Jordan.
- *c.*715 The rebuilding of the Al-Aqsa Mosque in Jerusalem is completed by al-Walid I. According to tradition the original Al-Aqsa Mosque was built in *c.*644.
- 724–27 Umayyad Caliph al-Hisham (reigned 724–43) builds the desert palace of Qasr al-Hayr al-Gharbi in the Syrian desert.
- 743–44 Umayyad Caliph al-Walid II (reigned 743–44) builds the palace of Mshatta in Jordan.
- 762 Madinat al-Salam (the 'City of Peace'), later called Baghdad, is founded by Abbasid Caliph al-Mansur (reigned 754–75) beside the river Tigris in Iraq.

Above *The interior of the Dome of the Rock is decorated with applied stucco work.*

- *c.*775 The fortified palace of Ukhaydir is built near Kufa, 200km (125 miles) from Baghdad.
- 775–85 Abbasid Caliph al-Mahdi (reigned 775–85) is the first Islamic ruler to put his name on official coinage.
- 784–86 Umayyad ruler Abd al-Rahman I (reigned 756–88) begins construction of the Mezquita in Córdoba, Spain.
- 805 Abbasid Caliph Harun al-Rashid (reigned 786–809) founds a public hospital in Baghdad. It is the first such institution in the Islamic world: within a few years many major cities in the Abbasid Empire have a public hospital named *bimaristan* (a Pahlavi word meaning 'place of the sick').
- 817–63 The Great Mosque at Kairouan, Tunisia, is built.
- 830 The Bayt al-Hikma ('House of Wisdom') – a library and centre for the translation of classical texts – is established in Baghdad by Abbasid Caliph al-Mamun (reigned 813–33).
- 836 Abbasid Caliph al-Mutasim (reigned 833–42) establishes a

new royal capital at Samarra, on the river Tigris.
- 848–52 Abbasid Caliph al-Mutawakkil (reigned 847–61) builds the Great Mosque of Samarra, with its spiral minaret.
- *c.*850–70 Muhammad al-Bukhari (810–70), a scholar resident in Samanid Bukhara (now in Uzbekistan), compiles the Sahih Bukhari, a collection of *hadith*, or sayings, of the Prophet Muhammad, that is considered the most authentic of all extant books of *hadith*.
- 859 The Qarawiyyin *madrasa* is established in Fez in Morocco. This is the oldest known *madrasa*.
- 886–940 Abbasid vizier Ibn Muqla (886–940) identifies the 'Six Pens' or classic scripts of calligraphy: *naskhi, muhaqqaq, thuluth, rayhani, riqa* and *tawqi*.
- 892 Abbasid Caliph al-Mutamid (reigned 870–92) returns the capital to Baghdad from Samarra.
- 892–943 A brick tomb is built in Bukhara (now Uzbekistan) to honour Samanid ruler Ismail Samani (reigned 892–907).

- 921 Fatimid leader Ubayd Allah al-Mahdi Billah builds the palace city of Mahdia on the coast of Tunisia.
- c.935 Iranian poet Rudaki (859–c.941) is active at the court of Samanid ruler Nasr II (reigned 914–43).
- 936–940 Umayyad Caliph Abd al-Rahman III (reigned 912–61) builds the city of Madinat al-Zahra near Córdoba in Islamic Spain.
- c.955 A woven silk textile now known as the Shroud of Saint Josse is made for Samanid official Abu Mansur Bukhtegin (d.960).
- 959 A *madrasa* is set up alongside the al-Azhar Mosque in Cairo, Egypt. This eventually develops into the prestigious al-Azhar University.
- 969 The Fatimids found the city of Cairo as a royal capital in Egypt.
- 1006–7 The Gunbad-i-Qabus tomb tower is built in Gurgan, Iran, for Ziyarid ruler Qabus ibn Wushnigr (reigned 978–1012).
- 1009–10 Iranian poet Firdawsi compiles his 60,000-couplet epic, *Shahnama* (Book of Kings).
- 1012 The Mosque of al-Hakim is completed in Cairo.
- 1033 Fatimids under Caliph Ali al-Zahir (reigned 1021–36) rebuild the Al-Aqsa Mosque in Jerusalem in the form it retains today. The mosque had been damaged by an earthquake.
- 1065 The al-Nizamiyya *madrasa* is set up in Baghdad by Seljuk vizier Nizam al-Mulk (1018–92). It is the first of a series of *madrasas* he establishes in Iran.
- 1078–79 The Ribat-i Malik *caravanserai* is built on the road between Bukhara and Samarkand (now in Uzbekistan) by the Qarakhanid Sultan Nasr (reigned 1068–80).

- 1082 The Great Mosque of Tlemcen (in Algeria) is built by Almoravid leader Yusuf ibn Tashfin (reigned 1060–1106).
- 1086–87 Nizam al-Mulk, vizier for Seljuk Sultan Malik Shah (reigned 1072–92), builds the south *iwan* (hall) at the Friday Mosque of Isfahan, Iran.
- 1088–89 Taj al-Mulk, Malik Shah's imperial chamberlain, adds the north *iwan* to Isfahan's Friday Mosque.
- c.1096 Fatimid vizier Badr al-Jamali rebuilds Cairo's city walls; he constructs the fortified gates of Bab al-Nasr and Bab al-Futuh.
- 1096 The Almoravid Great Mosque of Algiers is completed.
- 1125 Fatimid vizier Mamum al-Bataihi founds the Aqmar Mosque in Cairo.
- 1132–40 Norman King Roger II of Sicily (reigned 1130–54) builds the Palatine Chapel in his royal palace in Palermo.
- 1135-46 The Grand Mosque in Zavareh, central Iran, is built. It is one the earliest surviving mosques built with four *iwans,* or vaulted halls, opening on to the courtyard.
- 1142 The Mosque of Taza in Algeria is founded by Almohad leader Abd al-Mumin (reigned 1130–63).
- 1147-48 The Gunbad-i-Surkh tomb tower is built in Maragha, Iran, by architect Bakr Muhammad.
- 1154 Moroccan geographer Muhammad al-Idrisi (1100–66) completes his celebrated world map, probably the most accurate made during the medieval period. It is called the 'Tabula Rogeriana' because it is made for King Roger II of Sicily at his court in Palermo.
- 1157 The Mausoleum of Sultan Sanjar, is built at Merv (now in Turkmenistan).
- 1158–60 Another Seljuk four-*iwan* mosque is built at Ardestan, Iran.
- 1169 Zangid ruler of Syria Nur al-Din (reigned 1146–74) commissions four Aleppo craftsmen to make a beautiful new *minbar* for the Al-Aqsa Mosque, Jerusalem. It is installed in 1187 after Ayyubid general Salah al-Din takes the city.
- 1172–98 In Seville, Spain, the Almohads build the Great Mosque, which later becomes the city's Christian cathedral.

Above Inscriptions from the Quran were carved into the red sandstone of the Qutub Minar, a tall minaret in Delhi, India.

9

- 1176–83 Ayyubid ruler Salah al-Din builds the Citadel on Muqattam Hill, Cairo.
- 1190 Ghurid Sultan Ghiyath al-Din Muhammad builds the Minaret of Jam in Afghanistan. It is 60m (197ft) in height.
- 1193 Qutb-al-din Aybak – Turkic Muslim general and self-styled Sultan of Delhi – begins construction of the Qutb Minar in Delhi to mark the triumph of Islam in India.
- 1199 The *Kitab al-Diryaq* (Book of Antidotes) is one of many exquisite books made for the Zangid rulers of Mosul (Iraq). Zangid Mosul is also celebrated for its metalworking at this time.
- 1227–34 Abbasid Caliph al-Mustansir (reigned 1226–42) is responsible for the building of the Mustansiriya *madrasa* in Baghdad. It is designed with three *iwans* that lead on to a central courtyard.
- 1229 Anatolian Seljuk Sultan Ala al-Din Kaykubad I (reigned 1220–37) builds a *caravanserai* on the road from Konya to Aksaray, Turkey.

He builds a second *caravanserai* on the road between Kayseri and Sivas (also in Turkey) in 1232–36.
- *c.*1240 The Mosque of Djénné is built in Mali, western Africa.
- 1242–44 The *madrasa* of Ayyubid ruler Sultan al-Salih Najm al-Din Ayyub (reigned 1240–49) is built in Cairo.
- 1251 The Karatay *madrasa* in Konya, Turkey, is built by Anatolian Seljuk vizier Jalal al-Din Karantay.
- 1267–69 The Mosque of Mamluk Sultan Baybars (reigned 1260–77) is built in Cairo, Egypt.
- 1269 In what is now Somalia, the first Sultan of Mogadishu builds the Mosque of Fakhr al-Din. This is the oldest mosque in East Africa.
- *c.*1270 The second Ilkhanid ruler of Iran, Abaqa Khan (reigned 1265–82), builds the summer palace of Tahkt-i Sulayman in north-western Iran.
- 1284–85 The mausoleum and *madrasa* complex of Mamluk sultan Qalawun (reigned 1279–90) is built in Cairo. In 1284, Sultan Qalawun also builds the al-Mansuri Hospital in Cairo.

- *c.*1285 Ilkhanid ruler Arghun Uljaytu builds a new capital called Sultaniyya near Qazvin, north-western Iran.
- 1295–1303 The *madrasa* and Mausoleum of Mamluk Sultan al-Nasir Muhammad (reigned 1293–94, 1299–1309 and 1309–41) is built in Cairo, Egypt. It is begun by Sultan al-Adil Kitbugha (reigned 1294–96) prior to his deposition in 1296. Kitbugha installs the Gothic portal, brought from a crusader church in Acre (now Israel).
- 1309 The eighth Ilkhanid ruler of Iran, Uljaytu (reigned 1304–16), adds an exquisite stucco *mihrab* to the winter *iwan,* or hall, of the Friday Mosque in Isfahan, Iran.
- 1322–26 The ninth Ilkhanid ruler of Iran, Abu Said (reigned 1316–35), builds a congregational mosque at Varamin, Iran.
- 1327 The Djinguereber Mosque is built in Timbuktu, Mali, western Africa. It is the oldest of three ancient mosque-*madrasas* in the city; the others are the Sidhi Yahya and the Sankoré mosques, and the three together form the University of Sankoré.
- 1335–36 Mamluk Sultan al-Nasir Muhammad builds the Sultan's Mosque within the Citadel, Cairo.
- 1348–91 Nasrid sultans of Granada, Yusuf I (reigned 1333–54) and Muhammad V (reigned 1354–59 and 1362–91), expand the Alhambra Palace, building the Comares Palace and Palace of the Lions.
- 1356 Mamluk Sultan al-Nasir al-Hasan (reigned 1347–51 and 1354–61) commissions the building of his mosque and *madrasa* complex in Cairo.
- 1396–1400 Ulu Çami (the Great Mosque) is built in Bursa,

Above 14th-century tilework on the walls of one of the tombs in the Shah-i Zinda Mausoleum in Samarkand, Uzbekistan.

north-western Turkey, by Ali Neccar on the orders of Ottoman Sultan Bayezid I (reigned 1389–1402).

- 1399–1404 Turkic ruler Timur (Tamerlane reigned 1370–1405) oversees the construction of the Bibi Khanum Mosque in Samarkand (now in Uzbekistan).
- 1403 Timur builds the celebrated Gur-e Amir tomb complex in Samarkand.
- 1415–20 The Mosque of Mamluk Sultan al-Muayyad Shaykh (reigned 1412–21) is built in Cairo. It is the last Mamluk congregational mosque of monumental dimensions.
- 1417–21 Ulugh Beg, grandson of Timur, (reigned 1411–49) builds a fine *madrasa* in Samarkand to complement the one he constructs in Bukhara at the same time.
- 1459–73 Mehmet II begins building the Topkapi Palace, also in Istanbul.
- 1463–70 Mehmet II builds the Mehmet Fatih Kulliye in Istanbul. It contains a mosque, mausolea, hospital, *caravanserai*, a bathhouse, two *madrasas*, a library and soup kitchen.
- 1515 The Great Mosque of Agadez in Niger, western Africa, is built by Askia Muhammad I, ruler of the Songhai Empire (reigned 1492–1528).
- 1539–40 Safavid Shah Tahmasp I (reigned 1524–76) commissions two very large Persian carpets for the dynastic shrine at Ardabil, Iran. Both are dated and signed by Maqsud Kashani.
- 1543–48 Ottoman architect Mimar Sinan (1489–1588) builds the Sehzade Mosque in Istanbul.
- 1550–57 Mimar Sinan builds the Süleymaniye Mosque in Istanbul for Sultan Suleyman I

Above In this fine example of a 13th-century Mamluk Quran, the decorations are highlighted in gold, silver and lapiz lazuli.

'the Magnificent' (reigned 1520–66).

- *c.*1567–73 The young Emperor Akbar commissions an outsize manuscript of the romance *Hamzanama,* with 1,400 paintings.
- 1562 Mughal ruler Akbar (reigned 1556–1605) builds the Tomb of Humayan in Delhi to honour his father Humayan (reigned 1530–40 and 1555–56), second ruler of the dynasty.
- 1565–73 Akbar rebuilds the Red Fort of Agra, India.
- 1568–74 Ottoman architect Mimar Sinan builds the Selimiye Mosque in Edirne, Turkey.
- 1569 Akbar builds a new capital at Fatehpur Sikri, India.
- 1603–19 Safavid Shah Abbas I (reigned 1587–1629) builds the Lutfallah Mosque as part of his redevelopment of Isfahan, Iran. He also builds a Congregational Mosque on the same square, in 1611–30.
- 1612–14 The Tomb of Akbar (reigned 1556–1605) is built at Sikandra near Agra, India.

- 1609–16 Ottoman Sultan Ahmet I (reigned 1603–17) builds the Blue Mosque in Istanbul.
- 1632–54 Mughal Emperor Shah Jahan (reigned 1628–58) builds the Taj Mahal as a memorial shrine for his favourite wife, Mumtaz Mahal.
- 1656 Shah Jahan completes the building of the Jama Masjid Mosque in Delhi.
- 1678–82 The Ottoman Khan al-Wazir is built in Aleppo, Syria.
- 1706–15 The Shah Sultan Husayn mosque-bazaar complex is built on the Chahar Bagh in Isfahan.
- 1749 Ottoman governor Asad Pasha al-Azem builds the Azem Palace in Damascus.
- 1836 In Istanbul, Krikor Balyan completes the Nusretiye Mosque for Ottoman Sultan Mahmud II (reigned 1808–39).
- 1848 Muhammad Ali Pasha, Wali of Egypt, completes the grand Muhammad Ali Mosque in Cairo.
- 1855 Architects Garabet Amira Balyan and Nigogayos Balyan complete the Dolmabahçe Palace in Istanbul for Ottoman Sultan Abdulmecid I (reigned 1839–61).

- 1961 The Dhahran International Airport in Saudi Arabia is completed, designed by American architect Minoru Yamasaki.
- 1971 The Shayad Tower ('Memorial of Kings') is built in Tehran, Iran. After the Islamic Revolution (1979) it is renamed the Azadi (Freedom) Tower.

Below The Islamic world extended across Africa, Europe and Asia.

- 1973 The Great Mosque of Niono in Mali, western Africa, is completed using traditional techniques and materials.
- 1984 The Freedom Mosque in Jakarta, Indonesia, is completed by Indonesian architect Frederick Silaban.
- 1986 The King Faisal Mosque is completed in Islamabad, Pakistan. The architect, Vedat Delakoy, is Turkish.
- 1989 Architect Abdel-Wahed el-Wakil completes the King

Above During the 20th century, the 16th-century Iznik tiles on the Dome of the Rock were replaced with replicas.

Saud Mosque in Jeddah, Saudi Arabia.
- 1990 Architect Rasem Badran completes the King Abdullah Mosque in Amman, Jordan.
- 1993 The King Hassan II Mosque in Casablanca, Morocco, is finished. It is designed by French architect Michel Pinseau. Its minaret, at 210m (689ft), is the world's tallest.
- 1999 The Kingdom Tower office and retail complex in Riyadh, Saudi Arabia, is completed. It is 311m (1,020ft) tall. A rival Riyadh tower, the Al Faisaliyah Centre, is completed in 2000.
- 1999 The Burj al-Arab ('Tower of the Arabs') hotel is completed on a man-made island off Dubai.
- 2007 The Rose Tower built in Dubai. At 333m (1,093ft) tall, it is the world's tallest hotel.

Opposite An illustration of the city of Baghdad, showing the famous bridge of boats across the Tigris, from a 1468 anthology by Nasir Bukhari.

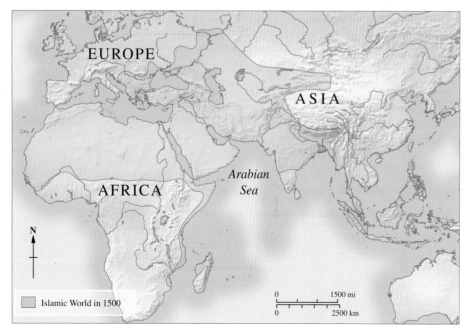

EUROPE

ASIA

Arabian Sea

AFRICA

N

Islamic World in 1500

0   1500 mi
0   2500 km

MANUSCRIPTS AND PAINTINGS

This chapter describes how the
Holy Quran has been a focus
for Islamic art across the
centuries, from the earliest
calligraphy and copies of the
text through to teams of artists
creating beautiful luxury
manuscripts. The chapter also
looks at the great paintings and
artists of the Islamic world.

*Opposite A painting of the Battle of Karbala, showing
Husayn's half-brother, Abbas, heroically defeating
an Umayyad soldier.*

*Above In later Qurans, the margins were often filled with
lavish borders. This 18th-century manuscript was
commissioned by the Sultan of Morocco.*

CALLIGRAPHY

THE MOST HIGHLY ESTEEMED ART FORM IN ISLAMIC CULTURE IS CALLIGRAPHY, PRIMARILY BECAUSE OF ITS SIGNIFICANT ROLE IN TRANSCRIBING THE WORD OF ALLAH, AS WRITTEN IN THE QURAN.

By reproducing the Quran's holy words, the calligrapher was held in the highest respect – far above other crafts and specialist artistic skills. The honour accorded for copying out a text of such spiritual and legal importance reflected the great responsibility of such a task. The writing itself also took on a spiritual quality, as did the *qalam*, or reed pen; in fact, one of the chapters of the Quran is called *Surah al-Qalam*, or 'the Pen'.

A scribe should always pray before commencing the copying of Quranic verses, which should be reproduced without any adulteration whatsoever. Important demands were also made of the Arabic script itself: it had to be legible, respectfully beautiful and unambiguous, worthy to record the word of God. Calligraphic reforms were undertaken in the 10th and 11th centuries on this basis: improvement to the legibility and gravitas of the written Quran was not only spiritually meaningful, but politically expedient.

ARABIC SCRIPT

One of the earliest Arabic scripts, used in the first Qurans, is usually referred to as *kufic*. Initially, art historians linked it exclusively with the Iraqi city of Kufa, but this is no longer considered the case. It is a dense rectilinear script, which was often written without the use of diacritics (marks appended to letters) or other conventional orthographic signs, so it could be difficult to read and potentially lead to variant readings of the authoritative sacred text.

In the 10th century, government reforms in Baghdad corrected this issue, and a new *khatt al-mansub*, or proportioned script, was developed under the supervision of the vizier (minister) Ibn Muqla (886–940). Six canonical cursive (joined-up) scripts emerged, known as the *sitta qalam*, or 'Six Pens', and these became the standard repertoire of a professional calligrapher. By the 11th century, cursive script was considered good enough to be used to copy out the

Above This page of Persian verses copied in nastaliq *script by Mir Ali of Herat was decorated and mounted in a 17th-century Mughal Indian album known as the* Minto Album.

Quran: the earliest extant example was executed in *naskh* by the calligrapher Ibn al-Bawwab.

LEARNING CALLIGRAPHY

Calligraphy was only taught to an apprentice by a master. The student had to learn to reproduce the canonical scripts with perfection, with absolutely no variance from the script of the teacher. The moment of graduation was usually the point when the student could truly replicate his master's hand. Great calligraphers kept proud note of their lineage from renowned masters, down generations of teachers and students. For example, the famous calligrapher Yaqut al-Mustasimi (d.1298) had six pupils, later known

Left This page from a 9th-century Quran was written in kufic *script on vellum; it has an illuminated gold roundel in the margin.*

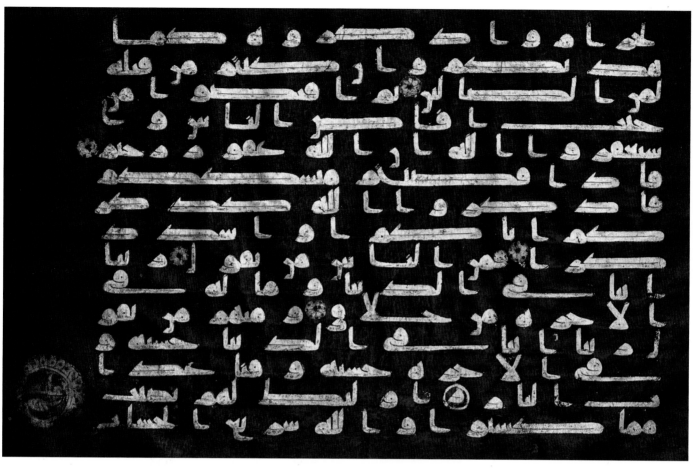

Above A page from a unique 10th-century Quran, known as the Blue Quran, was written in gold kufic script on indigo-dyed vellum.

simply as *sitta*, or 'the Six', from whom calligraphers in Timurid, Safavid and Ottoman times could still trace their descent.

As Islam spread across Western Asia, Arabic script was adopted to write other languages used in the wider Muslim world, such as Persian and Ottoman Turkish. Slight adaptations were necessary to provide new letter forms for Persian and Turkish sounds that did not feature in Arabic, such as 'ch' and 'v'. The fine art of calligraphy continued to be practised in the written literature of these other languages, and indeed a Persian calligrapher, Mir Ali, is credited with inventing a new style of (Arabic) script, entitled *nastaliq*, or hanging *naskh*. This elegant,

Above The thuluth *script around the neck of this mid-14th-century enamelled glass mosque lamp aptly quotes the Surah of Light from the Quran.*

somewhat italicized script became the characteristic mode for Persian poetry.

A DECORATIVE ART

The art of the pen was not limited to the written page, and calligraphy is found in almost every decorative medium: quotations of Quranic verses on a mosque façade, poetry on a jade drinking cup and informative details about the object's production, such as a patron's name, the artist's signature or the date it was made. Playful script also appeared in the decorative arts, such as 'knotted *kufic*' with plaits or braids adjoining letters, or anthropomorphic text that features human faces peering out from tall letters. The beauty of the script and the prominence of epigraphy demonstrate that text was not just literally informative but also important to the decorative value of the object.

OTTOMAN CALLIGRAPHY

DURING THE OTTOMAN PERIOD, SHAYKH HAMDULLAH AND OTHER OUTSTANDING CALLIGRAPHERS REFINED SEVERAL CALLIGRAPHIC SCRIPTS, EVEN CREATING A NEW OFFICIAL SCRIPT CALLED *DIWANI*.

Over the centuries, calligraphy became the foremost Islamic art form, a way of giving physical and visible form to the words of Allah as revealed to the Prophet Muhammad and recorded in the Quran. Calligraphers were highly honoured at the Ottoman court: the foremost Ottoman calligrapher, Shaykh Hamdullah (1436–1520), was befriended by the future Sultan Bayezid II when Bayezid was a prince in Amasya, and on Bayezid becoming sultan in 1512, he was summoned to Istanbul. According to tradition, Bayezid was happy to see himself as a pupil of Hamdullah, and willingly held the *hokka* (ink pot) while his master wrote.

SHAYKH HAMDULLAH

While at Bayezid's court, Shaykh Hamdullah created a new character and style for the *thuluth, naskhi* and *muhaqqaq* styles of calligraphy, in particular succeeding in making *naskhi* script unambiguous to read.

According to a tradition originating with Ibn Muqla, 10th-century vizier in Abbasid Baghdad, there were six 'hands', or canonical scripts: *naskhi, muhaqqaq, rayhani, tawqi, riqa* and *thuluth*. Shaykh Hamdullah's work in Istanbul was based on a close study of the writings and calligraphy of a 13th-century follower of Ibn Muqla named Yaqut al-Mustasimi (d.1295), who was revered in the Ottoman era as a master of calligraphy. Shaykh Hamdullah was hailed as Kibletul Kuttab ('Highest of scribes') and founded his own school of calligraphic artists in Istanbul. His followers greatly developed the *naskhi* script for use in copying books.

In the late 17th century, Hafiz Osman (d.1698) worked in the same traditions. He made further improvements to the *naskhi* script by drawing together the works of Yaqut al-Mustasimi and Shaykh Hamdullah. Such was

Above Some fine Ottoman calligraphy is displayed on the water fountain just outside the Topkapi Palace.

the stature of this calligrapher that he was hailed as Sayhi Sani ('the second Shaykh', a reference to Shaykh Hamdullah). His work had a great influence on later calligraphers.

A SCRIPT FOR DOCUMENTS

Ottoman calligraphers developed a new calligraphic style known as *diwani*, which was used for decrees, resolutions, endowments and other official documents. It was named *diwani* because it was used for the official documents of the sultan's *diwan*, or council of ministers. Only a few official calligraphers were instructed in this difficult script. The style was developed in the 16th century and was known to Shaykh Hamdullah – an album of his calligraphy preserved in the Topkapi

Left This elegant calligraphic line above a doorway at the Topkapi Palace reads: 'There is no god but God, and Muhammad is his Prophet.'

Above Verses from the Quran, inscribed in magnificent calligraphy, sanctify the walls and dome of the Süleymaniye Mosque in Istanbul.

Palace contains writing in the *diwani* script as well as in *naskhi, thuluth, muhaqqaq,* Riqa and Tawqi.

Ahmet Karahisari (1468–1556) was another leading calligrapher of the 16th century, a contemporary of Shaykh Hamdullah and a favoured artist at the court of Suleyman I 'the Magnificent' (reigned 1520–66). Karahisari was celebrated for his calligraphic representation of the *basmalah* formula in praise of Allah, which could be inscribed without lifting the pen from the paper.

Two splendid illuminated copies of the Quran largely composed by his hand are kept in the Topkapi Palace. One of these is very large, measuring approximately 61cm by 43cm (24in by 17in), bound in black leather with gilded ornament, and has 300 pages. It is written in the *naskhi, thuluth, muhaqqaq* and *rayhani* styles. The calligraphy, illumination and binding of this Quran are all of the highest quality, and it is viewed as an absolute masterpiece. However, this Quran was not signed by Karahisari, which is unusual. For this reason, textual historians believe that when Karahisari died in 1556 the work was unfinished, and that it was

probably completed by his adoptive son Hasan Celebi, who was another fine calligrapher.

DECORATIVE CALLIGRAPHY

Leading calligraphers also played an important role in other arts, providing designs for textiles, metalwork and ceramics, and notably sacred architecture. Ahmet Karahisari designed the grand calligraphic inscription in the dome of the Süleymaniye Mosque in Istanbul, built in 1550–57. In the same building, Hasan Celebi made a calligraphic piece above the harem door; the same artists produced fine work in the Selimiye Mosque in Edirne, built by Sinan in 1568–74 for Selim II.

THE SULTAN'S SEAL

Each Ottoman sultan had his own *tughra*, a calligraphic form of his name and title, with the words *al-muzaffar daiman* ('ever victorious') used as a signature and seal on official documents and on all coins issued in a sultan's reign. The calligraphy was increasingly embellished with infilled illumination, such as the spiralling foliate style, known as *tughrakesh*.

Above The tughra *of Sultan Murad III (reigned 1574–95) also appears over the Imperial Gate of the Topkapi Palace.*

THE QURAN

THE HOLY QURAN, WHICH CONTAINS THE TRANSCRIBED WORDS OF
ALLAH AS RECEIVED BY THE PROPHET MUHAMMAD IN 610–32, HAS
BEEN A FOCUS FOR ISLAMIC ART AND CULTURE ACROSS THE CENTURIES.

Over 22 years, beginning in 610, the Prophet Muhammad received 114 divine revelations through Jibril (the angel Gabriel). The revelations are collected in the Quran, which Muslims believe to be the complete and faithful record of what Muhammad was told. The teachings he received from Jibril – who is also referred to as the 'Spirit of Holiness' (Surah al-Nahl: 102) – are understood by Muslims to be the actual words of Allah.

Muhammad did not write the Quran (according to tradition he did not read or write). He passed on the words of Allah orally, repeating the revelations he had received to his early followers, who memorized them and passed them on to others.

SINGLE DOCUMENT

Scribes did write down some of the revelations using available materials, such as parchment, palm leaves, stone tablets and even animal bones. In these cases, Muhammad is believed to have had the records read back to him to check that the scribes had accurately written down his words. However, no attempt was made to gather the

revelations into a comprehensive written document until after Muhammad's death in 632. The situation changed when, in the Battle of Yamama (633) between Abu Bakr and followers of self-styled Prophet Musaylimah, at least 700 men who had memorized the Quran were slain. Leading Muslims saw the pressing need to make a written version for future generations before all those who had known the Prophet and his teachings at first hand had died.

A WRITTEN QURAN

One of the principal scribes, Zayd ibn Thabit (c.611–56), gathered the written revelations and wrote down all those existing in only memorized form. The results were approved by the *ashab* (Prophet's Companions) as being an accurate record of Muhammad's teachings. In *c.*654, during the era of Caliph Uthman ibn-Affan (reigned 644–56), a standardized version was drawn up and sent to the four cities of Kufa, Madinah, Damascus and Basra.

Some secular scholars claim that this traditional Islamic account of the collection of the Prophet's

Above Jibril transmits the words of Allah to the Prophet in this image from the Siyer-i Nebi, *an epic biography detailing the Prophet's life.*

teachings in the Quran is incorrect and that the book was gathered from various sources over centuries. For Muslims, however, it is a binding obligation of their faith that the Quran contains the words of Allah as received by Muhammad, full, complete and unchanging.

STRUCTURE

The Quran contains 114 suwar (singular surah), or 'chapters', each containing one of the revelations received by the Prophet. They vary greatly in length: some have 3 *ayat* (singular *ayah*), or 'verses', and some as many as 286. A chapter heading will usually indicate the number of verses in the chapter, and also the location of revelation: some were received in Makkah, and others in Madinah after Muhammad and the Muhajirun made the *hijrah* (migration). The revelations received in Makkah are generally shorter and are often mystical in character; those that were received in Madinah are longer and many

HISTORICAL QURANS

Fragments of the Quran found during restoration of the Great Mosque of San'a' in Yemen in 1972 have been carbon-dated to 645–90, so do certainly date back to this time. These pages are laid out in horizontal format and written in a slanting script called *Hijazi*. One remarkable page depicts an arcaded building which could be an Umayyad mosque. These fragments may be remains of variant forms of the book that were in existence before the standardized version was sent out by Uthman. This early painting is a unique example of an illustration in a Quran manuscript. Normally the Quran is never illustrated, because of the sacred primacy of the original written text.

revelations from Madinah appear before the earlier ones from Makkah. According to the Sunni tradition, Jibril dictated the order to Muhammad, and this gives the book an added, esoteric layer of meaning that pleases Allah but is not immediately apparent to readers. In the Shiah tradition, before the Quran was standardized under Uthman, the first Imam, Ali ibn Abi Talib, had a written version of the book made, and this was in a different order; but subsequently Ali accepted the order of the official Uthman version.

Above Muslim students study the Quran word by word. In Mali, Africa, a student copies a passage from the holy book on to a reusable wooden board.

give detailed practical guidance on ethical and spiritual matters. All the chapters, except *surah* 9, begin with the phrase of dedication known as the *basmalah*, 'In the name of Allah, most Beneficent, most Merciful'.

The material in the Quran is arranged in order of length, with the longest revelations first, with the exception of the first surah al-Fatiha. This means that the longer, later

ARABIC RECITATION

In the 7th century, many of the Prophet's contemporaries in Arabia were skilled in memorizing and reciting poetry. Muhammad passed on his revelations to his followers, who taught them to others through public recitation. Muslims today are encouraged to memorize the Quran and believe that its words are meant to be spoken aloud and heard by the faithful. The way the words sound is an important part of their effect on believers, which is why Muslims believe they should be recited in the language in which the revelations were given – Arabic.

Above A Bangladeshi girl recites a passage from the Quran in Arabic, the original language in which the revelations were given.

HOLY BOOK

The Quran is revered in book form. Some beautifully produced manuscripts or hand-written copies of the Quran are among the greatest of all Islamic works of art, with elegant calligraphy on the finest quality paper, verse markers and chapter headings in gold and coloured illumination, within skilfully worked leather bindings. Moreover, the very fact that the holy words of Allah can be physically bound within a book gives Muslims a deep reverence for books in general. The Quran is often quite simply referred to as al-Kitab, or 'the book'.

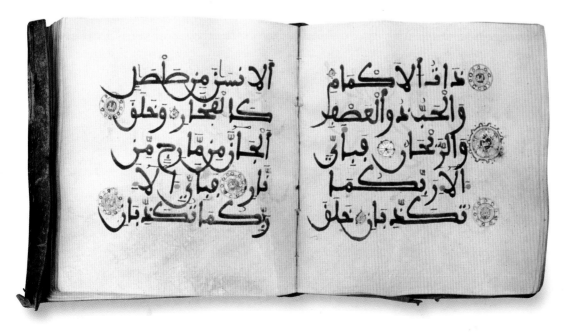

Left This Quran was made in North Africa in 1344.

EARLY QURANS

THE FORMAL SPLENDOUR OF ARABIC CALLIGRAPHY DEVELOPED WITH THE COPYING OF THE QURAN. INITIALLY WRITTEN IN A STIFF ANGULAR SCRIPT, IT WAS GRADUALLY REPLACED BY ROUNDER STYLES.

Although the Quran was revealed orally, the practice of copying its sacred text dates from the mid-7th century, when Caliph Uthman Ibn-Affan, who reigned from 644 to 656, sent out standardized versions to all the main Islamic strongholds.

REFINED CALLIGRAPHY

In their quest to emphasize the wonder of the sacred word, scribes took ever-increasing pains to adorn the holy text of the Quran. Like all scribes at that time, they used delicate pens, cut from dry reeds, varying the sharpness of the grooved nibs, according to the type of script that was employed.

The earliest Qurans were normally copied on vellum (dressed animal hide), usually sheepskin. This was gradually superseded by paper in the 7th and 8th centuries, when Muslims learned the art of paper technology from China.

KUFIC SCRIPT

The predominant angular style is often called *kufic*, although it is no longer associated with the Iraqi city of Kufa from which it took its name, and, more recently, codicologists have termed the style 'early Abbasid' instead. This script was written with an elegant, imposing hand, notable for its bold, angular appearance.

In its simplest form, the letters have a strong horizontal bias, rarely descending below the baseline. There are few Qurans dateable to the 7th century, but contemporary inscriptions on architecture and epigraphic coinage show that this measured formal style was well established. However, over the years more decorative forms of the script evolved. With 'foliated *kufic*', which became popular in Egypt, the tips of the characters were adorned with leaf or palmette shapes. Similarly, 'floriated *kufic*'

Above However fragmentary, ancient copies of the Quran are treated with great respect.

combined the letters with floral motifs and rosettes. During the 10th century, angular scripts were gradually superseded by more legible, rounded scripts, which had previously been restricted to more mundane and secretarial use. At the same time, paper technology had improved to the degree that it could also be used for Qurans for the first time.

IBN MUQLA

Rounded Arabic script reached a new peak of refinement during the time of Ibn Muqla (886–940), who is often hailed as the father of Arabic calligraphy. A vizier and chancery secretary in Abbasid Baghdad, he is credited with the proportional system of writing based on geometric principles known as *al-khatt al-mansub*, or proportioned writing. His precise

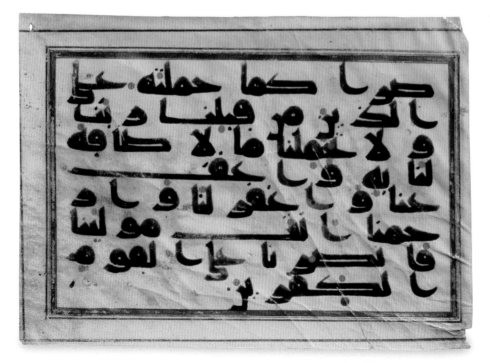

Left Early Qurans were written on horizontal leaves of parchment. The format of the page was echoed in the long, horizontal strokes of the kufic *script.*

IBN MUQLA'S DOWNFALL

The ordered nature of Ibn Muqla's calligraphy was not echoed in other areas of his life. He had a tempestuous political career, serving under three caliphs, but became embroiled in bitter conflicts with his rivals. Following one of these disputes, his right hand was severed as a punishment, although it is said that he learned to write equally well with his left. He ended his days imprisoned and disgraced.

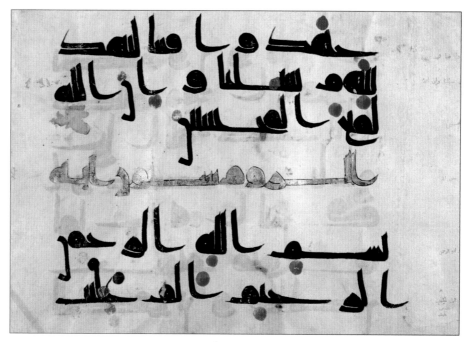

and perfect handwriting led one contemporary, al-Zanji, to compare Ibn Muqla's skill to 'the (God-given) inspiration of the bees, as they build up their cells'.

Later, Ibn Muqla's reforms became associated with the establishment of six canonical scripts, the 'Six Pens': *naskh*, *muhaqqaq*, *thuluth*, *rayhani*, *riqa* and *tawqi*. These are organized in three pairs of large and small versions: *tawqi* and *riqa*, *thuluth* and *naskh*, *muhaqqaq* and *rayhani*. (Today, *naskh* is the style most commonly employed in everyday use across the Arab world.)

IBN AL-BAWWAB

Ibn al-Bawwab ('Son of the Doorkeeper') was the greatest calligrapher of the Abbasid period. An outstanding copyist and regarded as a paragon of skill, he was an illuminator as well as a scribe, using his

Right This striking 14th-century Quran uses two different scripts for the text and for the surah- or chapter-headings.

artistic talents to endow the proportioned script established by Ibn Muqla with a rhythmic flow and elegance. He also wrote a very influential treatise on calligraphy, stressing the importance of measure, balance and spacing. It is believed that Ibn al-Bawwab completed 64 Qurans, but only one has survived into modern times. This Quran is held in the Chester Beatty Library in Dublin, Ireland. Dating from 1000–1, it combines Ibn al-Bawwab's inimitable smooth script

Above A page from a 9th-century Quran, written in kufic *script.*

with his sumptuous array of floral and geometric illumination. His rare talent elevated *naskh* script to a new standard, which made it acceptable to write out the Quran in this style for the first time. In the same period, paper also reached a new technical quality – the Dublin manuscript is the earliest known Quran manuscript written in *naskh* script, and on paper pages.

THE ART OF THE QURAN

ISLAMIC CALLIGRAPHERS DEVELOPED A REPERTOIRE OF FUNCTIONAL YET DECORATIVE DEVICES AS THEY COPIED THE SACRED TEXT, TO HELP NAVIGATE AROUND THE QURAN AND ALSO BEAUTIFY IT.

With the spread of Islam, the text of the Quran inspired some of the world's greatest artworks. Together, calligraphers and illuminators created some of the finest manuscripts ever produced. From the first, the main emphasis was on the beauty and clarity of the written word. As a result, calligraphers enjoyed a higher status than other artists.

EARLY SIGNS AND SYMBOLS

From the outset, the text of the Quran was adorned with a number of markings. Many of these were orthographic signs, added above and below the letters to indicate short vowels, doubled letters and other features of spelling.

In early Qurans, these signs could also indicate variant readings of the text, and they were written in up to four different colours: red, yellow, green and blue. In addition, there were a variety of symbols positioned at the end of verses and chapters, which were designed to help readers navigate their way around the text. In the earliest manuscripts, these symbols could be simple – the end of a verse, for example, might be marked by a cluster of gold dots. However, over the years these adornments grew more elaborate.

CHAPTERS AND VERSES

The text of the Quran is divided into 114 suwar (literally 'degrees', sing: surah), or chapters. From around the 9th century, the headings of these suwar became an important focus for decoration. In most cases, this took the form of an inscription in a decorative, rectangular frame, or *unwan*, specifying the title of the surah, the number of its verses and the site of its revelation (such as Makkah or Madinah). The inscription often featured a different script or colour than the one used for the main body of the text, usually *kufic* or *thuluth*.

Above The title of each surah was written in a different style to the main text and contained within a rectangular frame, as in this 12th-century example.

In the margin adjoining the frame, the illuminator sometimes added a palmette, a hasp ornament to emphasize a break in the text.

Some suwar received more attention than others. The pages relating to the first two, known as al-Fatihah and al-Baqarah, were always especially ornate. Surah al-Fatihah is short, filling just a page, and often recited as a prayer. The two suwar therefore begin on the same page opening. In later Qurans, the entire text of this initial section was enclosed in decorative borders, and the calligraphy itself was superimposed on a background of swirling patterns.

Illuminators also focused on the breaks between the *ayat* (sing: *ayah*), or verses, which made up these suwar. This provided a useful guide for those reciting the text, because the verses were of varying lengths. Different symbols were used, but rosettes or *shamsahs* (sunbursts)

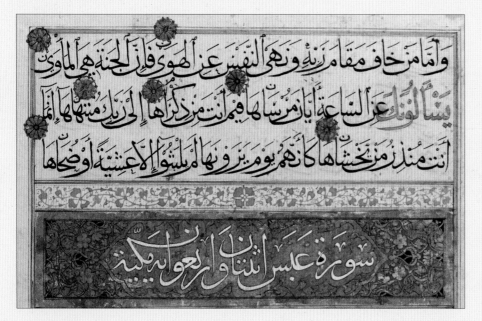

Left In the most expensive Qurans, the decorations were highlighted in gold, silver and lapiz lazuli. This 13th-century manuscript from Egypt is a particularly fine example.

were common. In addition, artists added more elaborate symbols in the margins, to denote every fifth and tenth *ayah*. These symbols mainly took the form of circular rosettes or tear-shaped medallions, with a brief inscription in the inner roundel.

OTHER DECORATION

Many Quran manuscripts also contained marginal designs, which were used in the passages to indicate where ritual prostration was required. Here, the word *sajdah* was inscribed in an ornamental setting. There was no

Below In later Qurans, the margins were often filled with lavish borders. This 18th-century manuscript was commissioned by the Sultan of Morocco.

Above A double-page section from a 14th-century Quran produced in North Africa. The ayah divisions are marked by rosettes and the script is Maghribi.

fixed format for this marking, although medallions and stars were popular choices. A more unusual variation can be found in a Mamluk Quran commissioned by Sultan Barquq. Here, the *sajdah* inscriptions were contained in a tiny image of a mosque.

LATER ERAS

The space given over to illumination in Quran manuscripts continued to expand and from the 14th century, extraordinary double pages of pattern were created. Some of these pages were designed to list the number of verses contained in the individual volume (the text of the Quran was frequently divided into 30 separate volumes).

Qurans were still copied out by hand in the 19th century, many years after the advent of printing, and calligraphers continued to use classic archaic scripts, such as *kufic* and *thuluth,* after they were no longer in general use.

MAMLUK QURANS

THE ART OF PRODUCING ILLUSTRATED MANUSCRIPTS OF THE QURAN REACHED NEW HEIGHTS DURING THE 13TH CENTURY, WHEN THE MAMLUKS CAME TO POWER.

From the mid-13th century, the Mamluks and the Ilkhanids were responsible for producing some of the largest and most lavish Qurans ever made. The overriding trend was to produce grander, more ornate manuscripts.

Mamluk Qurans often opened with a double-page frontispiece of lavish illumination. In addition, the calligraphers increasingly opted for large, dramatic scripts, such as *muhaqqaq* or *thuluth*.

RELIGIOUS FOUNDATIONS

The most sumptuous Qurans were not normally produced for the private use of wealthy patrons. In fact, these large-scale Qurans were usually commissioned for a religious institution, such as a mosque or a *madrasa* (religious college) founded by a particular amir or sultan. Their precise purpose was often set out in a *waqf*, a type of endowment set up to fund a religious or charitable purpose:

the Baybars *khanqa waqf*, for example, specifies that the Quran should be read each day at noon.

THE BAYBARS QURAN

An ambitious Mamluk amir, Baybars al-Jashnagir, briefly ruled as sultan in 1309–10. He built a charitable *khanqa* (Sufi residence) in Cairo, which was completed in 1309. Baybars commissioned a magnificent seven-volume Quran for his new foundation, now in the British Library. The Quran volumes are dated 1304–6 and represent the Mamluk arts of the book at their very best. The text is written in gold *thuluth* script and was copied by a famous calligrapher, Ibn al-Wahid (1249–1311), who had trained with the Baghdad master Yaqut al-Mutasimi (d.1298). An anecdote suggests that this renowned calligrapher could behave in a slightly underhand manner: Baybars once paid Ibn al-Wahid 1,600 dinars to copy out a new Quran –

Above Beautiful calligraphy in gold enhances this Mamluk Quran. It is at the Smithsonian Institution in Washington, DC, USA.

he spent only 400 on materials, pocketing the rest. Baybars' mild response was simply to ask: 'When will there be anyone else who could write out a Quran like he can?' Two renowned illuminators worked on the Baybars Quran: Ibn Mubadir decorated volumes one, two, four and six, while Abu Bakr – better known as Sandal – designed and executed the illumination in volumes three, five and seven. Both signed their work. Ibn Mubadir may have worked on Ilkhanid Quran projects, but it seems certain that he trained in Baghdad. The illuminator Sandal was famous among his contemporaries. He developed a delicate but ordered style of decoration, which was to influence a future generation of illuminators. This is most evident in his frontispieces, which usually took the form of a central star polygon, surrounded by elaborate trelliswork

Left The frontispiece of volume one of Sultan Baybars' seven-volume 1304 Quran – one of the most magnificent Islamic manuscripts.

infilled with palmettes. Several other Mamluk Qurans are signed by or attributed to Sandal. Little is known about the artist himself, except that he held a high position and may have been a eunuch. This particular detail is indicated by his name, Sandal or 'sandalwood': fragrant nicknames were typically given to eunuch slaves.

ILKHANID INFLUENCES

The Mamluk illuminators were undoubtedly influenced by some Ilkhanid trends, perhaps because Iraqi-trained artists like Ibn Mubadir were moving to Cairo. Influence is often attributed to two famous Ilkhanid Qurans. The first of these was a 30-volume Quran produced in 1313 in Hamadan for Sultan Uljaytu (reigned 1304–16), which was sent to Cairo in 1326, probably as a gift for the Mamluk Amir al-Nasir Muhammad. This was too late to have influenced the 1304–6 Baybars Quran in any way. The second, a Quran commissioned by Sirghitmish al-Nasiri, arrived in Egypt in the 1350s, and immediately made an impact. It was written in the *muhaqqaq-jali* script, a form that was instantly copied by Mamluk calligraphers. *Muhaqqaq* script uses shallow, sublinear curves with mid-line curvatures that extend horizontally, forming compact words that sweep toward the left.

The Ilkhanid influence on Mamluk Qurans was not confined to the lettering but can also be seen in the artwork. Chinese motifs played an increasing role in manuscript decoration,

Above This Quran casket, inlaid with brass and silver, is from 14th-century Egypt.

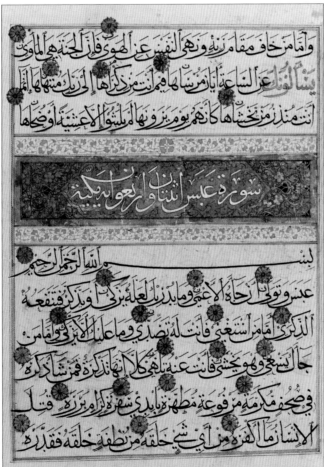

Above This Mamluk Quran has wonderfully elegant calligraphy and decoration, around the surah heading, in gold and pigments.

especially in the large, ornate frontispieces. Many of these had been decorated in the margin with a band of floral patterns, featuring peonies, lotus buds and other oriental blooms.

STAR POLYGON GROUP

Very fine Mamluk Qurans were produced in Cairo between 1363 and 1376, during the reign of Sultan Sha'ban. These include a number of manuscripts known collectively as the Star Polygon group. These manuscripts were named after their exquisite frontispieces, which were constructed around the radiating points of a star. A second group encompasses the work of Ibrahim al-Amidi, who was the most celebrated illuminator of the age. He used spectacular geometric designs, with unusual colour combinations and a broad range of motifs.

ILKHANID QURANS

WHEN THE ILKHANIDS CONVERTED TO ISLAM IN THE LATE 13TH CENTURY, THEY BEGAN PRODUCING QURANS OF THE HIGHEST QUALITY. THEY WERE THE FIRST TO PRODUCE MULTIVOLUME SETS.

Above A 14th-century Quran illuminated by one of the great Ilkhanid masters, Muhammad ibn Aybak. The complex geometric design is typical of his work.

The Mongol invasions of the 13th century marked an important development in Islamic culture. The death of the last Abbasid caliph in 1258 must have felt like the end of an era. At the same time, the change in regime opened up new possibilities, bringing direct contact with Chinese civilization, and introducing stability and wealth.

MULTIVOLUME QURANS

The new Qurans were created on a grander scale than anything seen before. The Ilkhanids pioneered a deluxe format, spreading the text over several volumes. Traditionally, the Quran has 30 sections, each of which is known as a *juz*. Ilkhanid manuscripts often devoted a separate volume to each of these sections, boxing them together in a container known as a *rabah*. Other divisions of the text can be found, ranging from 2 to 60 volumes.

By enlarging the format, the Ilkhanids offered new opportunities for both calligraphers and illuminators. Most volumes opened with an ornamental, double-page frontispiece and, in some cases, there was an additional decorative endpiece. The calligraphy, too, was far more impressive, as various types of monumental cursive script, using flowing joined-up letters, were

Below A 14th-century Quran copied in muhaqqaq script – this particular type was often used for Ilkhanid Qurans.

adopted. These included different combinations of *muhaqqaq, thuluth, rayhani* and *muhaqqaq-jali*.

The new regime did not, however, sever all connections with the past. The greatest calligrapher of the age was Yaqut al-Mustasimi (d.1298), a Turkish eunuch who had worked

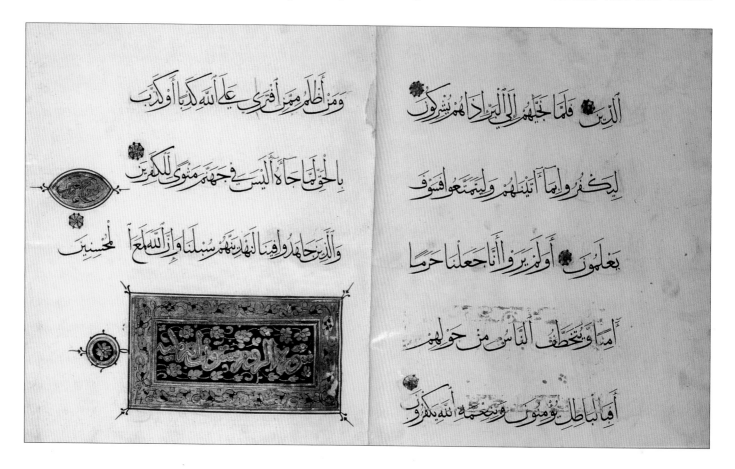

for the last caliph of Baghdad. He is said to have trained six gifted pupils, collectively known as the *sitta*, who preserved and transmitted his style during the Ilkhanid period. Although there is disagreement over the precise identity of some of these calligraphers, they are usually listed as Arghun ibn Abdallah al-Kamili, Nasrallah al-Tabib, Zarin-Qalam ('Golden Pen'), Yusuf al-Khurasani, Gandah-Navis and Shaykh-Zadah.

ULJAYTU AND THE QURAN

The most important Ilkhanid Qurans were produced in Iraq and western Iran, in the early 14th century. The chief patron was Sultan Uljaytu (reigned 1304–16). He founded a new capital at Sultaniyya, which he chose as the site of his elaborate mausoleum, now in ruins. Uljaytu commissioned a magnificent, 30-volume Quran for the memorial. Dating from *c.*1307–13, the manuscript is unusually large at 71cm by 51cm (28in by 20in) and features outstanding calligraphy. The script is mainly *muhaqqaq* or *muhaqqaq-thuluth*, and the lettering alternates between black outlined in gold, and gold outlined in black. The illuminator was Muhammad ibn Aybak, who displayed a preference for complex geometric compositions, with overlapping diamonds, circles and stars.

Uljaytu commissioned a number of other influential Qurans. These include another 30-part manuscript, which was produced in Mosul but was probably destined for the mausoleum in Sultaniyya. In this instance, both the calligraphy and the artwork appear to have been carried out by the same man, Ali ibn Muhammad al-Husayni. At the same time, Uljaytu also ordered a Quran from the Iranian city

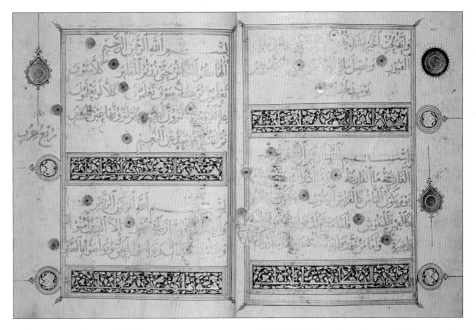

of Hamadan. This appears to have been commissioned as a gift, because the manuscript was sent to Cairo, where it caused a stir in Mamluk circles. The style is different from Uljaytu's Iraqi Qurans. The script is *rayhani*, and the decoration, in predominantly blue and gold, is simple but elegant.

PATRONAGE FROM A VIZIER

The other major patron of the period was Uljaytu's vizier, Rashid al-Din. He commissioned or

Above Calligraphers increasingly opted for more monumental styles of script and made the marginal symbols more ornate.

collected hundreds of Qurans, but, unfortunately, only a few fragments of these have survived. The most significant one was produced in Tabriz and is now housed in the Topkapi Palace.

Below This early 14th-century Ilkhanid Quran is copied in stately muhaqqaq script, written in gold ink, with illuminated panels.

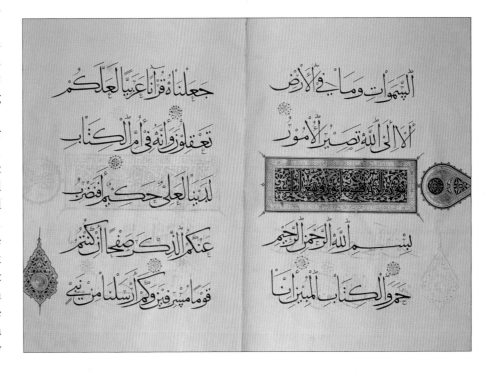

ILKHANID MANUSCRIPTS

IN THE LATE 13TH CENTURY, THE ILKHANID RULERS SPONSORED
MANUSCRIPTS THAT HIGHLIGHTED MONGOL LEGITIMACY ALONGSIDE
THE HISTORICAL AND LEGENDARY KINGS OF THE WORLD.

After the rulers of the Ilkhanid dynasty converted to Islam in the late 13th century, they set about establishing their cultural legacy as legitimate rulers of the Islamic world. They did this by writing their own history and appending it to older accounts of world history. Many notable illustrated works were produced, including the Compendium of Chronicles and 'The Great Mongol *Shahnama*'.

A WORLD HISTORY

The grandest of these projects was ordered by Ghazan Khan (reigned 1295–1304), who commissioned a multivolume universal history from his minister Rashid al-Din (d.1318).

Below Rashid al-Din's universal history included an account of the Islamic world: this section illustrates the Samanid dynasty of Iran, showing Mansur b. Nuh coming to the throne in 961.

The location of this endeavour was the Rab-i Rashidi precinct, which was founded by Rashid al-Din himself, north-east of the Ilkhanid capital Tabriz. This vast personal suburb included a mosque, the patron's tomb, a Sufi hospice, a hospital (Rashid al-Din was also a royal physician), library and teaching facilities, with over 300 employees. The scale of this foundation is relevant to the magnitude of the universal history project, which was ambitious.

Entitled *Jami al-tawarikh*, or Compendium of Chronicles, the work comprised the history of Ghazan Khan and the Mongols, a world history describing the Arabs, Jews, Turks, Persians, Indians, Franks and Chinese, and a geography volume. Earlier works of history had to be assembled from across the known world, translated and collated together, and, in order to

Above Produced in c.1330 Ilkhanid Tabriz, this Shahnama *painting shows Shah Bahram Gur, a legendary marksman, out hunting onager.*

do this, an international team of scholars was formed, as well as copyists and painters.

According to the foundation documents, two large copies of this compendium were to be produced every year, one in Arabic and one in Persian, and dispatched to different cities of the Ilkhanid realm,

either Arabic- or Persian-speaking. The completed work was officially presented to Ghazan's successor Uljaytu in 1310, but it was an ongoing project of systematic and centralized production.

Densely illustrated, the earliest extant copy is dated 1314, and is now divided between Edinburgh University Library in Scotland and the Khalili Collection, which is privately owned. The painting style is strongly influenced by Chinese illustrated narratives, and reflects the international resources available to artists at the Rab-i Rashidi, but also the quick pace imposed upon them. The project did not last more than a few years. In 1318, Rashid al-Din was accused of poisoning Uljaytu. Following his execution, his foundation and estates were plundered and the project ceased.

MAKING A STATEMENT
The Compendium of Chronicles presented an account of world history with the Mongol Empire positioned in a global context, ennobling their current supremacy in cultural terms. The dynasty also sponsored illustrated manuscripts of Iranian cultural heritage, thereby deliberately reasserting Iranian identity within the Ilkhanid court. The same tactic was applied by Qubilai Khan in Yuan China, where the Mongols also seized power in the 13th century. Dynastic histories were commissioned in order to enlist the support of the Chinese administrative elite.

'THE MONGOL *SHAHNAMA*'
To this day the *Shahnama* (Book of Kings) by the 11th-century poet Firdawsi remains the national epic of Iran, and the earliest illustrated copies were apparently produced in Ilkhanid centres. This classic poem is extremely long, and describes generations of kings and heroes of pre-Islamic Iran, in their ancient feud with neighbouring Turan. The political meaning of commissioning this text is evident: by promoting ancient Iranian kings, the Mongols were aligning themselves as worthy royal successors in a long and noble line. Several illustrated copies date from the early 14th century. From this point onward, it becomes a characteristic mode of kingship for Persian rulers to commission personal illustrated manuscripts of Firdawsi's work.

Above In 'The Great Mongol Shahnama', Alexander the Great orders the construction of massive iron walls to keep out the savage people of Gog and Magog (shown top left).

The manuscript known as 'The Great Mongol *Shahnama*' is a masterpiece of Ilkhanid painting, and was probably ordered for Abu Said in the 1330s. The paintings reflect some of Rashid al-Din's style, but have a deeper range of colour, more exciting compositions and a more dynamic range of figures recounting the adventures, tragedies and romances of Iran's ancient heroes. The manuscript contained at least 60 paintings. Today, these are dispersed in worldwide collections – due to the fateful decision made by a 20th-century art dealer to dismantle the book and sell the folios.

TIMURID MANUSCRIPT PAINTING

DURING THE 15TH CENTURY, THE TIMURID PRINCES OF IRAN SPONSORED THE PRODUCTION OF LUXURY MANUSCRIPTS. CLASSIC WORKS OF PERSIAN LITERATURE WERE MADE BY TEAMS OF ARTISTS.

In the late 14th century, the Turkic conqueror Timur sacked many of the great cities of the Middle East, and as he did so, he conscripted the skilled citizens of his conquests into his service at his capital of Samarkand. Centralizing cultural skills was beneficial to Timur's court, because the finest artists, calligraphers, poets, scholars and craftsmen of the day were assembled in one place. Timur's sons and grandsons were educated by an elite selection of masters, and grew up to be connoisseurs of the arts.

After Timur's death in 1405, the empire was subdivided among his male descendants. Timurid princes were posted as regional governors in several Iranian cities, where each

Above Humay arrives on horseback at the palace gates of his beloved Humayan, in an anthology produced in 1396.

had his own atelier, or workshop, of artists and calligraphers to produce illustrated manuscript copies of Persian literary classics. Different schools of Timurid painting style developed in Shiraz, Herat and Samarkand, under these various patrons, whose ambitious military rivalry was also played out in the cultural sphere. At the same time, a commercial industry of manuscript production developed for other wealthy members of society.

PRODUCTION IN HERAT
Baysunghur Mirza (1399–1433), one of Timur's grandsons, was a renowned patron, 'alike in talent and the encouragement of talent', as described by a court biographer. His court welcomed poets and artists. He died young, however, allegedly by falling from his horse while drunk. During his time, the

Left Humay recognizes Humayan in this woodland scene, produced by Junaid Sultani for this Jalayirid manuscript.

Right Muslim pilgrims perform the Hajj *at Makkah, in this Shiraz manuscript from c.1410–11. It was produced for the Timurid Prince Iskandar Sultan.*

exact workings of an atelier in Herat were recorded in a contemporary document, datable to the late 1420s. Entitled *Arzadasht*, this is a progress report apparently written by the atelier director Jafar al-Tabrizi for his patron, Baysunghur Mirza.

Jafar provided a list of more than 20 craftsmen, describing which project each was engaged with: these are calligraphers, painters, illuminators, gilders, bookbinders and leather workers. As well as the ongoing progress of manuscript production, Jafar described repair work and restoration of damaged manuscripts, preparation of designs to be given to craftsmen to decorate tent poles, saddles and ceramic tiles, and problems with staff illness.

Jafar's account shows how designs were produced centrally in Timurid art, and how they were applied to a range of different media. This systematic process of distribution explains the stylistic unity in Timurid art, in which designs and motifs recur with regularity.

It is also possible to see the high level of specialization practised among artists, and to get a glimpse at how a manuscript painting was created. One note specifies that the painter Amir Khalil had finished applying silver to a seascape in a *Gulistan* manuscript (silver was typically painted to represent water), and would now proceed to paint in the colours. Remarkably, this exact manuscript survives in the Chester Beatty Library in Dublin and, indeed, contains two seascapes.

INFLUENCE FROM BAGHDAD

The style of Timurid court painting was strongly influenced by the late 14th-century art of the Jalayirid dynasty from Baghdad and Tabriz,

and manuscripts that were illustrated at Baysunghur Mirza's court atelier are very similar to the exquisite crystalline style of Jalayirid works. Timurid princes not only admired Jalayirid manuscripts, but in the early 15th century, they employed the same artists: the painter Amir Khalil recorded in Baysunghur Mirza's *Arzadasht* had previously worked for Jalayirid rulers in Baghdad, and presumably, had been conscripted by Timur after he took the city in 1401.

In turn, some Late Timurid artists actually went on to work under the subsequent Safavid dynasty in the early 16th century, and so on. The continuity of the Persian painting style from the 14th century onward was clearly noted by the 16th-century commentator Dust Muhammad: in an album preface dated from 1544, he observed of an early 14th-century painter: '[the style of] depiction which is now current was invented by him'.

LATE TIMURID PAINTING: BIHZAD IN HERAT

THE PAINTER BIHZAD WORKED FOR THE TIMURID COURT IN LATE 15TH-CENTURY HERAT, AND IS CREDITED WITH CREATING A NEW AND INFLUENTIAL STYLE OF PAINTING.

In the second half of the 15th century, Timurid military power began to decline, and the dynasty lost western and southern territory to Turkman tribal confederations. The former empire was eventually reduced to the region of north-eastern Iran, where Sultan Husayn Bayqara (reigned 1469–1506) ruled over the last Timurid court in Herat. He was a legendary patron of cultural activity, and hosted an extraordinary coterie of scholars, poets and artists at his court. This included the calligrapher Sultan Ali Mashhadi, the poet Jami and the painter Bihzad, whose masterpieces were all admired and emulated for centuries. Husayn Bayqara's chief minister, Mir Ali Shir Navai, was also a poet, and the prince himself wrote literary debates.

Above Bihzad's illustration of Laila and Majnun meeting at school, from the Khamsa of Nizami *(1494–95).*

EVOLVING PAINTING STYLE

In this milieu, there came about a radical development in manuscript painting, which determined the character of Persian painting in both Iran and Mughal India for the following centuries. The style of depicting figures and landscape changed greatly, as did some of the typical subject matter. This has been characterized as a cool, rational and even humanistic approach, rendering figures in more natural poses and expressions, and using a more modulated palette of colour.

Credit for this change has been given to one artist, Kamal al–Din Bihzad (d.1535), but it is unlikely that he was the only artist to work in this new style. He was probably a leading proponent rather than a lone pioneer. His work bridges the end of the Timurid period and beginning of the Safavids, and his transfer from one court to the next ensured the continuity of Persian painting traditions, from Timurid to Safavid patronage.

Left Bihzad's illustration of Harun al-Rashid at the bathhouse, from the Khamsa of Nizami *(1494–95).*

Above Bihzad's depiction of Iskandar, or Alexander the Great, as he consults the seven sages, from the Khamsa of Nizami *(1494–95).*

As with all respected painters, Bihzad's style was imitated and his compositions were re-drafted by generations of Persian artists as a matter of course. Owing to this renown, 'signatures' of Bihzad may be found widely, inscribed on to paintings, perhaps by later owners making a hopeful attribution, or by painters feeling their work worthy of the great artist's name.

THE *BUSTAN*

The exact corpus of Bihzad's work is not fully agreed, but one of his least disputed works is the *Bustan* (or 'Garden') of the poet Saadi (d.1291), a luxury manuscript dated June 1488, which features five masterpiece paintings: one double frontispiece and four subsequent illustrations. Each illustration is discreetly signed by Bihzad, on a horseman's arrow quiver,

Right The royal herdsman reproaches Shah Dara, signed by Bihzad (1488).

on a hand-held book or placed in the calligraphic frieze around an architectural setting. The double frontispiece is a remarkable scene of feasting, no doubt revealing the world of Husayn Bayqara's famous court. The revellers are drinking heavily from wine cups, while servants are kept busy pouring from vessels of porcelain, glass and precious metal. A still is seen in operation on a hill beyond the courtyard.

By contrast, the dignified ruler kneels beneath an illuminated canopy, conversing with a younger courtier and listening to music. An upstairs window opens to reveal the prince's porcelain collection, giving further evidence of his refinement.

KHAMSA OF NIZAMI

A second manuscript generally agreed to be partly illustrated by Bihzad is a copy of the *Khamsa of Nizami*, dated 1494–95, now in the British Library in London. Typically of late Herati Timurid painting, the new subject matter of the 22 illustrations is a little more realistic than the typical jewel-like canon of earlier 15th-century works. They have added genre scenes of an old beggar woman and a busy building site, as well as a working bathhouse, with active figures engaged in their affairs, however humble they may be. These realistic vignettes contrast with the royal scenes of court society, and challenge their complacent, comfortable privilege.

SAFAVID MANUSCRIPT PAINTING

IN THE FIRST HALF OF THE 16TH CENTURY, A COORDINATED TEAM OF ARTISTS AND CRAFTSMEN AT THE SAFAVID COURT PRODUCED LUXURY MANUSCRIPTS OF EXCEPTIONAL QUALITY.

Above This illustration of Adam and Eve (c.1550) is from the Falnama, *a work of bibliomancy attributed to the sixth Shiah Imam, Jafar al-Sadiq.*

When the Safavid young crown prince Tahmasp was sent to Herat to be regional governor, his court there included the company of Herati artists from the last Timurid *kitab-khana*, or atelier (workshop), that of Sultan Husayn Bayqara. The renowned master painter Bihzad was head of the *kitab-khana*, and it was the young Tahmasp's privilege to be tutored by him.

When Tahmasp finally returned to the Safavid capital Tabriz in 1522, his taste for metropolitan Timurid painting would have been at odds with the current idiom of the Tabriz court atelier, which was directed by the painter Sultan-Muhammad in the Turkman style. However, Prince Tahmasp then studied under Sultan-Muhammad, while the elderly Bihzad was brought to Tabriz and appointed director. From this amalgamation, the placement of a Herati master at the head of the Tabriz painters, the character of 16th-century Safavid court painting was set, as a stylistic synthesis of taste, under a royal patron who was an able connoisseur of both modes, and a competent artist and calligrapher too. The results were spectacular.

TAHMASP'S *SHAHNAMA*

In 1524, Tahmasp became shah and soon after, from *c.*1524 to 1540, his court painters produced the grandest *Shahnama* (Book of Kings) manuscript ever seen. The manuscript has 258 paintings in its current state, most of which appear toward the beginning. It provides an extraordinary showcase of 16th-century Safavid court art, with recognizably Timurid or Turkman aspects, and a successful fusion of the two styles, where fluid figures are painted in finely detailed compositions, using brilliant rich colours.

Although there are few signatures or dates on the paintings, one – the remarkable *Court of*

Left A Shahnama *scene attributed to Sultan Muhammad shows the hero Faridun striking the tyrant Zahhak with an ox-head mace.*

Gayumars – has been identified as the work of Sultan-Muhammad from a description in a biography of the Tabriz master. The painting shows a crowded court scene set in a rocky landscape, but look closely and it is possible to see an astonishing array of minuscule faces and figures, barely discernible to the naked eye, concealed in the rocks and clouds. The biographer's description is effusive: '[he] has developed depiction to such a degree that, although it has a thousand eyes, the celestial sphere has not seen his like…With the pen of his fingertips, on the tablet of vision, he has drawn a different version at each and every instant.'

A POLITICAL STATEMENT

Firdawsi's epic poem tells the history of generations of pre-Islamic Iranian kings, from the dawn of time up to the last Sasanian shah. It consists of some 60,000 couplets and is packed with eventful narratives of suspense and derring-do, making it an ideal text for illustration. Being a royal commission, a king's personal copy of the *Shahnama* has political significance too, as it bestows the glamour of historical Persian kingship upon its owner – perfect for a Safavid shah, or any Iranian ruler.

It has been suggested that Tahmasp may have had additional motives for commissioning such an ostentatious version. In 1514, his father Ismail had been soundly defeated by the Ottomans at the Battle of Chaldiran. The Ottomans went on to sack the Safavid capital, Tabriz, including the royal treasury. As a key theme of the *Shahnama* is the Iranian triumph over their longstanding enemies, the Central Asian Turkic Turanians, this new version may have brought some solace to the Safavids in a post-Chaldiran world by enabling them to relive earlier victories over the Turks. Tahmasp may also have wanted to replace the *kitab-khana*'s losses after the Ottoman sack of the capital by commissioning a major new project.

THE SHAH'S DISAFFECTION

Tahmasp, his brother Bahram Mirza (d.1549) and Bahram's son Ibrahim Mirza (d.1577) were all bibliophile princes, with a connoisseur's eye and personal training in painting, calligraphy and poetry. They commissioned manuscript paintings, collected art and exchanged gifts, such as the precious 1544 album of paintings and drawings given to Bahram Mirza by his brother the Shah. The album is prefaced with an illuminating account of Persian art history as told by a 16th-century compiler named Dust Muhammad.

The history of Safavid painting took an abrupt turn around this time, due entirely to a change of heart on Tahmasp's part. He turned increasingly to religion throughout the 1530s and 1540s, renouncing non-Islamic habits, and gradually abandoned the company of his youth, dismissing from the Safavid court his artists, musicians and poets. They sought employment at

provincial courts and beyond in Mughal India, or simply retired.

In 1567, Tahmasp's monumental copy of the *Shahnama* was one of many spectacular accession presents sent to the new Ottoman ruler, Selim II, in the hope of retaining an important peace treaty agreed with Selim's predecessor Suleyman. In view of this decision, Tahmasp's apparent disaffection shows political

Above This scene from a 1536 Shahnama *depicts Khusrau ascending the throne.*

maturity. The biographer Qadi Ahmad notes: 'having wearied of the field of calligraphy and painting, [Tahmasp] occupied himself with important affairs of state, with the wellbeing of the country and tranquillity of his subjects.'

THE *KHAMSA* OF NIZAMI

REVERED AS ONE OF THE GREAT MASTERPIECES OF PERSIAN
LITERATURE, THE *KHAMSA* (QUINTET) WAS WRITTEN BY THE
12TH-CENTURY POET NIZAMI.

Nizami was the pen name of
Ilyas Yusuf Nizami Ganjavi
(1141–1209), who was born and
spent the great part of his life in the
south Caucasian city of Ganja, then
part of the Seljuk Empire and now
known as Gyandzha, in Azerbaijan.
He was orphaned early in life and
raised by his uncle, Khwaja Umar.

Nizami lived a simple, quiet life,
largely keeping away from court –
although he had a number of royal
patrons. He was a passionate
admirer of the early 11th-century
poet Firdawsi's *Shahnama* (Book of
Kings) and used it as his source for
material in his own epic. In
addition to the *Khamsa*, Nizami also
wrote many odes and lyrics, but few
of these have survived.

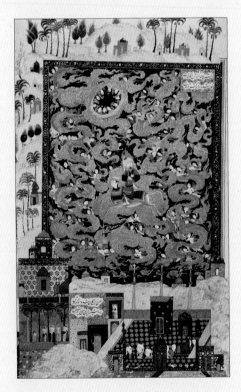

***Above** An illustration of the Ascension
of the Prophet Muhammad, as retold
in the* Khamsa, *dated 1505.*

THE FIVE PARTS

The *Khamsa* is an anthology of five
epic poems written between 1171
and 1202 in the *masnavi* style of
rhyming couplets (*masnavi* means
'the doubled one'). The poems were
dedicated by Nizami to local
dynastic lords and Seljuk rulers.
Comprising 30,000 couplets in
total, the work is known as the
Khamsa (the Arabic word for 'five').

The first of the five poems,
Makhzan al-Asrar (Treasury of
Mysteries), differs from the rest in
that it is not a romantic epic but a
collection of 20 parables on
religious and ethical themes, such as
the benefits of just royal rule and
the necessity for all to ready
themselves for life after death.
Written in 1171, the *Makhzan al-
Asrar* acknowledges its debt to an
earlier work, the *Hadiqat al-Haqiqa*
(Garden of Truths) of the 11th- to
12th-century Persian Sufi poet Sanai.

TWO ROMANTIC POEMS

Khusrau o-Shirin (Khusrau and
Shirin), the second of the five
poems, was written in 1177–80.
This is an epic treatment of
the celebrated story, also told in the
Shahnama and in other sources,
of the proud and protracted
courtship between the Sasanian
King Khusrau II and Princess
Shirin of Armenia. The pair fall in
love before they have even
met: Shirin by seeing Khusrau's
portrait, Khusrau by hearing Shirin
described by poets. The course of
the relationship is not smooth,
however, and the two endure
quarrels, separation and jealousy
before they finally agree to marry.

***Above** A scene from the* Khamsa
*(c.1550), showing a game of polo
between a team of men and a team
of women.*

Layli o-Majnun (Layla and
Majnun), completed in 1192, is the
third of the five poems, and
recounts a legend of tragic love
from Arab sources. A poet named
Qays falls passionately in love with
his cousin Layla at school, but
cannot wed her because of a family
quarrel and, as a result, is driven into
madness. His strange behaviour
wins him the name Majnun (from
the Arabic for 'mad'). He cuts
himself off from normal life,
isolating himself in the desert with
only wild animals for company and
writing love poems about Layla.
The star-crossed couple never find
union in life, but after death are laid
to rest in a single grave.

According to legend, the story
was based on real events that took
place in 7th-century Umayyad
Arabia: a Bedouin poet fell in love
with a young woman of his tribe,
the Bani Amir, but was refused her
hand in marriage by her father and
afterward isolated himself in the
Najd desert; his family left food in
places where they knew he would

find it. This story passed into the Persian tradition, and was recounted by the 9th–10th-century Persian poet, Rudaki.

EXPLOITS OF GREAT RULERS

The *Haft Paykar* (Seven Portraits, or Beauties), the fourth poem in the *Khamsa*, was completed in 1196 and recounts episodes from the life of the Sasanian King Bahram V (reigned 421–38), often known as Bahram Gur. While a prince, Bahram is sent to the court of an Arabian king. There, he discovers a secret room containing paintings of beautiful princesses from China, India, Africa, Russia, Turkistan, Byzantium and Iran, representing the seven regions of the world. Bahram learns that when king he will marry all seven princesses.

Once on the throne, Bahram sends out a messenger to find and bring back the seven princesses. Upon their return he has a palace built for each one where they are visited by the king. The central section of the poem is subdivided into seven tales, delivered as the seven stories told to Bahram Gur over seven consecutive nights by each of his seven brides.

Nizami acknowledged his debt to Firdawsi's *Shahnama*, where Bahram's exploits had already been described, but he also presented several adventures from the king's life that were not described by Firdawsi. Literary scholars hail this poem as Nizami's masterpiece.

The final epic in the *Khamsa* is the *Iskandar-nama* (Book of Alexander), written in 1196–1202, celebrating the many legendary and mysterious events from the life of Macedonian general, Alexander the Great (356–323BCE). The poem contains 10,500 couplets arranged in two books: the *Sharaf-Nama* and the *Iqbal-Nama*. The second book

focuses on Alexander's personal qualities, and his emergence as the ideal worldly ruler.

CLARITY AND LEARNING

The *Khamsa* is celebrated for its originality of expression and clear, colloquial use of language. It also shows Nizami to be a man of great learning, capable of drawing on both Persian and Arabic literary traditions, and of making references to astronomy, astrology, medicine,

Above A duel between two court doctors, a scene from Nizami's Khamsa, *copied in Tabriz c.1539–43.*

Islamic law, music, philosophy, botany, alchemy and mathematics. His work was very influential, and the *Khamsa*, a set of five epics, became a literary form in its own right. The Indian Sufi Amir Khosrow (1253–1325), and the Timurid statesman Mir Ali Shir Navai (d.1501) also wrote *khamsas*.

OTTOMAN MANUSCRIPT PAINTING

THE OTTOMANS AMASSED AN EXTRAORDINARY LIBRARY AT THE TOPKAPI PALACE. THE COURT ATELIER PRODUCED MULTI-VOLUME ILLUSTRATED MANUSCRIPTS OF OTTOMAN HISTORY AND GENEALOGY.

Above A painting (c.1475) of Mehmet the Conqueror at the height of his power, possibly by Sinan Bey.

To this day, the library of the Topkapi Palace houses a remarkable collection of manuscripts, acquired over four centuries by Ottoman sultans and their courts. Some sultans were known bibliophiles, such as Mehmet Fatih and Ahmet III, who built personal collections.

Exceptional books also came to the palace library as diplomatic gifts, and from the sacked treasuries of defeated powers. The Ottoman

Below This portrait of Sultan Selim II (reigned 1566–74) firing an arrow was painted by Nigari, one of the artists working at the Topkapi Palace, Istanbul.

military successes over the Mamluks of Egypt and Syria, as well as the Safavids of Iran, brought substantial riches, including manuscripts.

Books were given as important acts of international diplomacy, which indicates their status as major cultural assets. In 1567, the Safavid Shah Tahmasp of Iran sent a great consignment of gifts to Istanbul to congratulate the Sultan Selim II on his accession. The first two items on the list were books: the first was a copy of the Quran said to be handwritten by Ali, the Prophet's son-in-law, and therefore a sacred relic. The second was a two-volume copy of the *Shahnama* which was arguably the finest illustrated Persian manuscript ever produced. At the time, Ottoman taste favoured the styles of early 16th century Safavid Iran, which is evidenced by a lively export trade of manuscripts from commercial centres in Shiraz to the Ottoman empire. The Safavid court manuscript of c.1520–40 was an exceptional example, and constituted an appropriate gift to the Ottoman court, although it may also have implied a message about Iran's supposedly greater artistic heritage.

COURT PAINTERS

Working at the palace, the court painters may have benefited from the imperial library's holdings of illustrated books from east and west. The stylistic influence of Safavid Iran was important, but the court artists came from lands throughout the empire, as well as former Safavid territories.

Imperial patronage determined the types of manuscripts and paintings the atelier produced, and Ottoman illustrated manuscripts certainly reveal independent ideas which were not indebted to Safavid painting traditions. Court archives record how the artists' workshop was organized, and give details of names, salaries and ethnicity, as well as noting personal presentations of masterpieces, offered directly by the artist to the sultan on a festive occasion or bayram. The sultan would usually reward presentations with a gift of cash or robes.

IMPERIAL HISTORIES

The Ottoman sultans were keen to claim an important place in history, and establish their position as the

Left The 1541 reception of Hungarian
Queen Isabella and infant King Stephen
is depicted in this commercial manuscript.

Left The 1541 reception of Hungarian
Queen Isabella and infant King Stephen
is depicted in this commercial manuscript.

of the Sultan's death on his military
campaign, the funeral procession
and final burial in Istanbul. On a
municipal level, illustrated *Surname*
manuscripts also described the
public festivities accompanying
court celebrations as well as guild
processions through the city streets.

As Ottoman territory included
the two holy cities of Makkah and
Madinah, the Sultans promoted and
protected the pilgrimage routes,
and the facilities at the holy places.
This pious undertaking may be
related to the production of multivolume illustrated accounts of the
lives of the prophets in the late 16th
century, such as the illustrated 1594
six-volume manuscript of *Siyer-i
Nebi* (The Life of the Prophet).

Other biographies outline
the history of Islam from Adam
to the Prophet Muhammad and the
Caliphs and, by extension, to
the Sultans themselves. Prayerbooks
praising the two holy places were
produced, with topographical
illustrations of the pilgrim sites.

rightful successors to past Islamic
rulers and key religious figures. To
this end, they commissioned official
dynastic histories, genealogies and
portrait series.

Historical accounts of the
Ottomans were densely illustrated
and the paintings provide exciting
views of 16th-century court life.
For example, most of the reign of
Sultan Suleyman 'the Magnificent'
(reigned 1520–66) is described in
the *Suleymanname* (dated 1558),

written by the court panegyrist
Arifi. The biography is the final
volume in a series of five, dedicated
to the dynastic history of the
Ottoman sultans. A subsequent
book (dated 1579–80) provided an
addendum volume, covering the
remaining ten years of Suleyman's
reign: this includes dramatic scenes

Right The Procession of the Trade
Corporations was illustrated in Vehbi's
Surname, 1720.

Reza Abbasi

Regarded as the most important and influential Persian artist of the 17th century, Reza Abbasi (d.1635) specialized in playful portraits of Isfahan's people.

Reza's father was the court artist Ali Asghar, who had served successive Safavid shahs and princes in the late 16th century, at the courts in Qazwin and Mashhad. Following custom, he trained his son as a painter too, so Reza grew up in the company of the elite artists who had served at the royal ateliers (workshops) of Shah Tahmasp, Prince Ibrahim Mirza, Shah Ismail II and Shah Abbas I.

He showed talent at an early stage, and was strongly admired by his contemporaries, as was recorded in a contemporary biographical note: 'it is fitting that the present age should be proud of his existence, for in the flower of his youth, he brought the elegance of his brushwork, portraiture and likeness to such a degree that [the great artists of the past] would praise his hand and brush a hundred times a day. In this age he has no rival; master painters, skilful artists who live in our times regard him as perfect.' Shah Abbas was also appreciative of Reza's talent, awarding him the honorific title 'Abbasi' as a measure of his esteem.

PORTRAIT ARTIST

Reza specialized in the single-page paintings or tinted drawings that were in vogue in Iran in the late 16th century. This romantic genre features slightly windswept lone figures in an idealized natural setting. Reza contributed to at least one manuscript painting project at this period, but then he began his single-page portraiture, with great success. He focused on young courtiers relaxing, but also created powerful images of people in the wider community. His 1598 drawing of a portly official taking his turban off to scratch his head is a masterpiece of observation.

Above A fluid depiction of hunters in the landscape, painted by Reza Abbasi five years after he rejoined the royal workshop in 1610.

CHANGE IN CHARACTERS

In 1598, the Safavid court moved from Qazwin to Isfahan, which was transformed into a vibrant imperial capital thanks to major architectural and commercial projects initiated by Shah Abbas I. New palaces and mosques were built in this old city, as well as monumental public spaces, major avenues, garden quarters and bridges. A great part of Reza Abbasi's surviving works reflect the moneyed society of this new capital, with portraits of foppish youths and dallying girls dressed in high fashion and posed in relaxed mood, enjoying romantic picnics of wine and fruit.

However, in the period from about 1603 to 1610, it would seem that Reza tired of this company, for he withdrew from court circles and entered a different sphere of Isfahan life. This is recorded with

Left Reza Abbasi's satirical depiction of a young Portuguese merchant as he allows his dog to drink from his wine cup, painted in 1634.

Above *Sitting alone, this young woman adjusts her make-up. A young man woven into the design of her cushion cover seems to spy on her.*

disapproval by biographers of the day. One biographer notes: 'He avoided the society of men of talent and gave himself up to association with low persons', while another comments: 'vicissitudes [of fate] have totally altered Aqa Reza's nature. The company of hapless people and libertines is spoiling his disposition. He is addicted to watching wrestling and to acquiring competence and instruction in this profession.' Sure enough, Reza's portraits from this period typically depict wrestlers, dervishes and other humble characters that belonged to an Isfahan subculture not usually represented in court art.

This period of disaffection may have been triggered by Shah Abbas's departure on a military campaign against the Ottomans in 1603, when Reza was left behind in Isfahan and then wearied of the other remaining courtiers. After about 1610, the artist returned to Abbas's court and resumed his paintings of courtiers, although he also continued to portray older dervishes until his

Above *This alcove painting of a young woman, from the Ali Qapu Palace in Isfahan, is in the style of Reza Abbasi.*

death in 1635. The double portrait of a younger court dandy paired with an older, wiser dervish was a recurring theme in Reza's work, emphasizing the contrast in lifestyle and outlook of these two different sections of society.

A LASTING INFLUENCE

Reza's influence on contemporary artists was considerable; it lasted throughout the 17th century and can be seen in paintings, murals, ceramics and textiles. This is evident from the work of Reza's students, such as his son Shafi Abbasi and Muin Musavvir, and many other painters, including Muhammad Qasim and Muhammad Yusuf al-Husayni. In addition, there are a large number of 17th-century paintings that appear to be 'signed' by Reza, but which are in fact tributes made by later painters.

AFSHAR, ZAND AND QAJAR PAINTING

IN THE 17TH CENTURY, FOREIGN STYLES AND TECHNIQUES BEGAN TO INFLUENCE ART IN IRAN. EXPERIMENTS WITH WESTERN TECHNIQUES INCREASED DURING THE 19TH CENTURY UNDER THE QAJAR DYNASTY.

Later 17th-century Safavid art increasingly began to toy with international styles, such as Mughal themes, and European conventions, such as tonal modelling, perspective and the technique of oil painting.

The late 17th-century artist Muhammad Zaman produced unsettling illustrations of familiar subjects from the *Shahnama* and *Khamsa* featuring (European) classical architecture rendered in steep perspective. Full-length oil portraits were also produced at this time depicting single figures – not unlike the genre established by Reza Abbasi earlier in the century.

In 1722, an Afghan invasion overturned the Safavid dynasty, and the rest of the century was a dismal period of tribal violence and civil war. In 1736, Nadir Shah Afshar founded the shortlived Afsharid dynasty, which was followed in 1751 by that of the Zands. Karim Khan Zand established his capital in Shiraz. Several full-length portraits have survived from his reign, along with some of the early works of Mirza Baba, who is better known as a Qajar artist.

QAJAR IMPERIAL STYLE

Long-term stability returned when the Qajar dynasty came to power in 1794, led, with some brutality, by Aga Muhammad (d.1797). The Qajar capital was established at Tehran, which remains the capital of modern Iran today.

The distinctive Qajar style emerged during the long reign of Fath Ali Shah (1797–1834), Aga Muhammad's nephew, who commissioned a number of oil portraits of himself and his many sons. He used the portraits, which emphasize his full beard, large eyes and wasp waist and show him wearing heavily jewelled crown and regalia, to cultivate an imposing

Above The Qajar ruler, Nasir al-Din Shah, is shown wearing Western-style military uniform and sitting on a Western chair in this 1857 portrait.

Above This c.1805 portrait of Fath Ali Shah shows him wearing the jewelled crown of the Qajar dynasty.

Left The Qajar Empire reached its peak early in the reign of Fath Ali Shah (1797–1834), but later lost considerable territory to foreign powers.

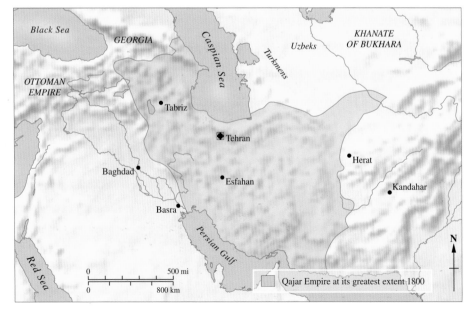

Black Sea

GEORGIA

Caspian Sea

OTTOMAN EMPIRE

Turkmens

Uzbeks

KHANATE OF BUKHARA

Tabriz

Tehran

Baghdad

Esfahan

Herat

Kandahar

Basra

Persian Gulf

Red Sea

| 0 | 500 mi |
| 0 | 800 km |

Qajar Empire at its greatest extent 1800

N

Above This Qajar oil painting of a dancing musician illustrates contemporary female fashions.

public image, and he had them distributed around Iran as well as sent abroad to a number of foreign rulers. Fath Ali Shah also commissioned an enormous mural for his Negarestan Palace in Tehran. Depicting an imaginary court reception to celebrate *No Ruz* (Persian New Year), it showed the shah surrounded by 12 of his sons, together with retainers and foreign ambassadors from Britain, France, the Ottoman Empire, Sind and Arabia.

THEMES IN QAJAR PAINTING
Qajar artists also produced paintings of beautiful women, including a series made for the Nigarestan Palace in Tehran. These ranged from royal women to dancers, musicians and serving girls. The most unusual subjects were the acrobats and tumblers who entertained the royal household, and are depicted upside down, balancing precariously on their hands, elbows and even on the tips of knives.

Right A ceramic tile showing musicians and dancers at the court of Qajar ruler, Nasir al-Din Shah.

As Iran moved into the modern era under Muhammad Shah (reigned 1834–48), Western-style reforms and fashions continued. Military uniform became formal dress at court, as can be seen in contemporary imperial portraiture.

The taste for Western art and culture remained strong during the long reign of Nasir al-Din Shah (reigned 1848–96), who made three official tours of the courts of Europe and was keen to present Iran abroad as a similar imperial nation. He was particularly taken with the new invention of photography and took it up as a hobby – building his own studio and taking up to 20,000 photographs of the court, including his mother, wives and children. His albums remain in the collection of the Gulestan Palace.

In 1851, Nasir al-Din Shah set up a European-style technical college in Tehran called Dar al-Funun (House of the Arts) to train military cadets, engineers, musicians, doctors and interpreters. Photography and lithography were also taught, which encouraged their wider use. Painting was added to the curriculum in 1861. In the later Qajar period, the Ghaffari family from Kashan produced generations of important court painters: Abu'l-Hasan Khan Ghaffari (d.c.1866), who had the title Sani al-Mulk (Craftsman of the Kingdom), was sent to Italy by Muhammad Shah to study academic painting and lithography. His nephew Muhammad Ghaffari (d.1940) was a major court portraitist who studied at Dar al-Funun and also spent five years in Paris.

LACQUER PAINTING

ISLAMIC LACQUER-PAINTED OBJECTS ARE RARE BEFORE THE 17TH CENTURY BUT BECAME VERY POPULAR IN THE LATE SAFAVID, QAJAR AND ZAND PERIODS.

In the Islamic world two different techniques were used to produce a lacquered surface. In the first technique, a resinous substance called 'lac' – which is produced by certain insects – was painted directly on to wooden objects. In the second, much more common technique, an object was first painted with an image in watercolour paint, then coated with a thin layer of protective varnish made from resin.

LACQUER BOOKBINDINGS
In Iran, lacquer painting developed during the late 15th century, when it was first adapted for use in Timurid bookbinding in Herat. The technique soon spread to Safavid Tabriz and other cities. Artists painted designs in watercolour on to a prepared surface of papier mâché, or pasteboard, then applied a coat of varnish, thus replacing traditional leather bindings. The varnish could be given an added sheen by carefully mixing it with powdered gold or mother-of-pearl.

The immediate stimulus for this activity came from new polychrome lacquers that had recently been imported from the East. The most influential of these was *qiangjin* – incised black lacquer infilled with gold. Islamic artists hurried to copy this gold-and-black palette. The popularity of lacquer bindings increased under the Safavids and reached a peak in the Qajar era.

Over the years, lacquer artists developed a varied repertoire of themes and design styles. There were simple, ornamental designs, composed of arabesques and scrollwork; elegant scenes of courtly entertainments in idyllic gardens; studies of birds and flowers; and, in the 19th century, rolling landscapes, influenced by European painting.

Royal portraits were also in demand, and a well-known Qajar lacquer binding depicts Fath Ali Shah taking part in a lively hunting scene.

Left A Qajar box from 1867, which depicts Shaykh Saadi in conversation with Nizami and his attendants.

Above This beautiful blue iris, painted by Muhammad Zaman in 1663–64, appears in a manual on bookbinding and lacquerwork.

AN EXPANDING ART FORM
From the 17th century, Iranian artists began applying lacquer decoration to a wider range of objects. Among the most popular uses were on pen cases. These elongated boxes carried all the accoutrements of the calligrapher's art – reed pens, an inkwell, a small, sharp knife for cutting fresh nibs and scissors to trim the sheets of paper. In the finest examples, painting was added to both the interior and exterior of the lid.

Later, in the Qajar period, the range of lacquered objects also included fans, mirror-cases, backgammon boards, musical instruments and playing cards.

Most lacquered objects were adorned with lyrical arrangements of butterflies, birds, and flowers, but some pieces were also decorated with narrative and popular historical scenes. One of the most spectacular items is an ornate chest dated 1840, now kept in the British

Museum in London. The box contains a collection of instruments for weighing jewellery, and its lid is painted with a colourful scene of King Solomon enthroned and surrounded by an array of *jinns* (genies), *peris* (angels) and *divs* (demons).

Another casket, by the leading court painter Muhammad Ismail, shows in minute detail the siege of Herat by Muhammad Shah on the top of the lid and other scenes from the same military campaign are painted around the sides.

19TH CENTURY

In terms of quantity, the 19th century was the high point of Iranian lacquer production. British orientalist, Sir William Ouseley, who spent two years working and studying in Iran from 1810–12, described in his writings seeing lacquered pen boxes, as well as mirror-cases and an array of caskets piled high in the bazaar. Many of these pieces were signed and dated by their artists. The leading family of lacquer painters during this time

Below These lacquer bookbindings, painted in 16th-century Iran, show a hunting scene (left) and a prince, under the awning, enjoying courtly life (right).

Above This Qajar lacquered papier-mâché pen case, from c.1880, shows Safavid ruler Shah Ismail defeating the Uzbeks in 1510.

was Muhammad Ismail, his brother Najaf Ali and his three sons. Many of their works were inspired by European subjects, but they also dealt with local political leaders, such as Manuchihr Khan, who is featured holding court on a lacquered pen box dating from 1840–50, which is held in London's Victoria and Albert Museum.

MUGHAL PAINTING

UNDER AKBAR'S LIBERAL PATRONAGE OF PERSIAN AND INDIAN PAINTERS, THE ART OF THE MUGHAL MINIATURE EVOLVED, REACHING PERFECTION AT THE COURT OF JAHANGIR.

From the 16th to 19th centuries, artists found almost continuous employment at the Mughal court. They even accompanied the rulers on their hunting expeditions and military campaigns. Akbar (reigned 1556–1605), although reportedly illiterate, had a passion for books, particularly illustrated ones. He had also been taught to paint as a child. Early in his reign, he established a large studio of talented indigenous artists, who worked under the direction of the two great Persian masters, Mir Sayyid 'Ali and Abd as-Samad, who had been brought back from Iran by Akbar's father, Humayun.

Artists learned their trade as apprentices, often from their fathers or uncles as the craft was frequently a family occupation. They were taught how to make paintbrushes from bird quills set with fine hairs, how to grind their pigments and how to prepare the aqueous binding medium of gum arabic or glue. Seated on the ground, with one knee bent to support the drawing board, they painted with opaque watercolour on paper or occasionally on cotton cloth.

NATURALISM

Under Akbar's close supervision, a style of manuscript illustration evolved that combined native Indian traditions – he particularly admired Hindu painters – with Persian technical refinement. These manuscripts were full of vivid representations of plants, flowers, animals and people, despite orthodox religious objections to figurative painting. As Akbar's official historian, Abu'l-Fazl, had commented: 'Bigoted followers of the letter of the law are hostile to the art of painting, but their eyes now see the truth.' This naturalism was also influenced by European prints and pictures brought to the Mughal court by merchants and Jesuit missionaries.

Above Beautiful mounts were a feature of Mughal painting. This example contains a portrait of Emperor Aurangzeb.

AKBAR'S MANUSCRIPTS

In about 1567, Akbar ordered his artists to prepare an illustrated copy of the *Hamzanama*, the story of the mythical adventures of the uncle of the Prophet Muhammad. A team of 100 painters, gilders and binders were assembled for the task. The multivolume work contained no less than 1,400 paintings and took 15 years to complete.

One of the most outstanding examples of the Akbari style was the *Akbarnama*, the official history of Akbar's reign written by Abu'l-Fazl. The vivid, naturalistic paintings illustrate scenes from the emperor's daily life and events from his military campaigns. At his death, Akbar's library contained some 24,000 volumes, including works in Persian, Arabic and Greek, many of which had been copied during his reign to the highest standards of book production.

Left A study of a zebra painted by the artist Mansur in 1621 for the famous 'Minto Album' begun by Jahangir. Exotic animals were commonly presented as diplomatic gifts.

JAHANGIR'S ARTISTS

Akbar's achievement as a patron of artists was refined under Jahangir (reigned 1605–27), who was a great connoisseur of the arts and claimed that he could distinguish the work of each of his painters at a glance. Preferring quality to quantity, and lacking his father's fondness for grand projects, he greatly reduced the staff of the royal studio, concentrating instead on a few favourite masters. As a result, fewer illustrated manuscripts were produced and more individual pictures, usually portraits or animal and flower studies, were created.

During this time, artists were encouraged to paint with increased realism and subtlety, softer colours and more harmonious designs. Much of this work shows the influence of European

painting, such as the use of perspective and shading. The individual paintings were often mounted in exquisitely decorated borders and bound together in albums. Many of Jahangir's artists continued to paint under his son Shah Jahan (reigned 1628–58), but the style changed. One of the last great Mughal historical manuscripts was the *Padshahnama*, a chronicle of the first ten years of Shah Jahan's reign that recorded military victories and court ceremonials. The paintings, although richly detailed, are more formal and lack the dynamism of those produced under Akbar and Jahangir.

Left Emperor Babur and his architect are shown planning the Bagh-i-Wafa near Jalalabad (1589–90).

ROYAL PORTRAITS

A large number of portraits were produced under Akbar. 'His Majesty himself sat for his likeness,' reported his chronicler Abu'l-Fazl, 'and also ordered to have the likenesses taken of all the grandees of the realm.' Jahangir's preference for individual pictures, rather than the historical manuscripts of Akbar's reign, also encouraged portraiture. His admiration for European art saw the beginning of a more naturalistic style of portrait. Toward the end of his reign, his portraits contained Islamic, Hindu and European imagery. Under Shah Jahan and his successors, portraiture became more stiffly official in character, as can be seen from the massed ranks of courtiers in the Padshahnama.

Above A likeness of Emperor Akbar (1542–1605), painted shortly after his death. He encouraged the artist to paint 'individual' works.

Above A portrait of Emperor Jahangir (1569–1627) holding a portrait of his father, Emperor Akbar (reigned 1556–1605).

COMPANY PAINTINGS

As the Mughal Empire began to decline, the emperor's patronage of artists was taken up by officers of the East India Company. These works are known as Company paintings.

The Mughal emperors were receptive to Western artistic ideas and both Akbar (reigned 1556–1605) and his successor Jahangir (reigned 1605–27) had collected European prints and other works of art. Mughal artists copied these imported pictures and began to paint nature with greater realism, adding shading and perspective to their own work.

EARLY COMMISSIONS

Both the Mughal love of nature and their penchant for portraits were shared by many Britons and Europeans based in India. The British were also familiar with the technique of Indian artists – opaque watercolour or gouache on paper – because it was identical to that used by artists in Britain. Having seen and admired the work of Mughal artists, in the mid-18th century officers of the East India Company began to commission their own paintings from them.

The initial commissions were for miniature paintings, executed in the traditional Indian manner but showing scenes with European figures. These portraits often depict a portly European gentleman, sometimes wearing Indian dress, seated awkwardly on a cushion and drawing on a *huqqa*, a type of smoking pipe. With their propensity for documenting everything, the British commissioned pictures of native crafts, castes, festivals and pastimes – indeed, exactly the kind of subjects that are photographed today. The depiction of natural history subjects and topographical views of famous Mughal monuments followed.

One of the earliest and most important collections of natural history subjects was commissioned in Calcutta between 1777 and 1783 by Lady Mary Impey, wife of the Chief Justice of Bengal. While the drawings show a mastery of the subject, they have a power and

Above Only a few Indian artists were known by name, but Dip Chand signed this charming picture of Dr William Fullarton on his terrace, puffing a huqqa.

character all their own. Their distinctive quality perhaps indicates that the artists were given complete freedom to express their talents as they wished.

THE FRASER ALBUMS

A remarkable collection of more than 90 watercolours by Indian artists was commissioned between 1815 and 1819 by two brothers, James and William Baillie Fraser. Known as the Fraser Albums, this collection is now generally accepted as one of the finest groups of Company pictures ever painted by Indian artists. They record a broad range of Indian life in Delhi and its surroundings and depict some of the colourful Indian characters encountered by William Fraser in the course of his civil and military employment. One of the most arresting drawings is of a young Indian trooper who had saved his life when he was attacked by a would-be assassin.

Left These two women and a buffalo were painted by the Indian artist who accompanied William Fraser on his travels for the East India Company.

Because the Indian artists were regarded by their patrons as no more than employees, few of their names were recorded. Most Indian painters were artists because they had been born into a family whose men followed the caste profession. Although the identity of the artists who worked on the Fraser Albums is uncertain, they are thought to be the work of a single family, that of Ghulam Ali Khan. He is probably also the artist responsible for the illustrations in the Skinner Album, commissioned by Colonel James Skinner, the Anglo-Indian Colonel of the famous Irregular Cavalry Corps, Skinner's Horse.

TOPOGRAPHICAL PAINTINGS

The first purely topographical artist known from late Mughal Delhi was Mazhar 'Ali Khan. It seems likely that he was commissioned by Thomas Metcalfe, the Agent representing British power at Delhi, to produce 125 paintings of Mughal monuments in the city and surrounding area. One of the most impressive of his pictures, painted in 1846, is a large-scale panorama of Delhi, nearly 5m (16ft) wide. It is a valuable record of the Red Fort and the outlying city before much of it was destroyed in 1858.

One well-known name among Indian artists working for the British in Calcutta was Shaykh Muhammad Amir of Karraya. His paintings depict the British way of life in and around the city: their large, palatial mansions, favourite dogs, horses and carriages. One picture, painted in 1845, shows a little girl on a pony attended by no less than three servants. Her face is entirely hidden by a blue bonnet and her isolation from reality seems to symbolize the colonial position of the British in India before the Mutiny that occurred in 1857.

Above The British often employed local Indian artists to paint their houses or favourite animals. This racehorse, jockey and groom are shown on the racecourse.

Above This bird of prey was one of 44 paintings, bound together in a volume, which were executed by an Indian artist for an East India Company botanist.

POTTERY, GLASS, TILES AND STONE

This chapter features a range of beautiful Islamic ornaments, describing the geometric patterns that decorate pottery and ceramics, the techniques for cutting, enamelling and gilding glassware, the use of individually painted tiles in mosaics, and the carved stonework in Islamic buildings.

Opposite This elaborate mudéjar ceiling, built after 1504, is in the monastery of San Juan de los Reyes, in Toledo.

Above The Ilkhanids were passionate about hunting. Birds and animals of the chase, such as these startled hares, were popular decorative themes.

ORNAMENT

ISLAMIC ART AND DESIGN WERE SHAPED BY CERTAIN RESTRICTIONS
ON THE DEPICTION OF THE LIVING IMAGE. THIS LED ARTISTS TO
DEVELOP STYLIZED FORMS TO GREAT EFFECT.

Figurative art, so important in the Christian tradition, has never been as significant to religious art in the Islamic world. Strictly-speaking, image-making has been linked to idolatry, and although there is indeed an historic Islamic tradition of portraying sacred figures, artists decorated religious architecture or objects with different types of design. On a broader level, Islamic art has a very refined design tradition, which extends further than figural subjects.

GEOMETRIC PATTERNS

Often understood as the most typical form of Islamic art, geometric design is used with great precision across the media, in art and architecture. Craftsmen utilized a simple repertoire of shapes – circles, squares, stars, lozenges, polygons – but assembled them in patterns of dazzling complexity.

Above An end-piece from a Quran of 1568, produced for the Sharifi Sultan of Morocco, includes complex patterns constructed around a simple, geometric shape – a radiating star.

Larger compositions could achieve the mesmeric effect of an optical puzzle, using complex radial symmetry. Similarly, in an architectural context, long stretches of geometric patterns could act as a fascinating surface, not necessarily reflecting the physical structure that lay beneath. The walls of the courtyard in the Yusuf madrasa at Marrakesh in Morocco provide a typical example.

Perhaps the most popular of these motifs was the star. Radiating stars were used as basic components in a huge variety of designs: from the colourful decorative panels in manuscripts, to an inlaid wooden panel or a glazed tile façade. Some of the most intricate examples can be found in Egyptian woodwork, especially in the ornate minbars (Islamic pulpits), where they were combined with ivory inlays.

An important three-dimensional form of geometric decoration was muqarnas, or stalactite vaulting, used throughout the Middle East. This was used to create a rich

Left A vaulted arcade from the carpet bazaar in Qom, Iran, displays waves of muqarnas decoration, rippling out from the apertures in the centre of each dome.

honeycomb effect in vaulted ceilings and archways. Celebrated examples can be seen in the halls of the Alhambra, in Granada, Spain.

ABSTRACT DECORATION

The Quran contains grave warnings against the production of idols for worship, and Hadith literature condemns the vanity of equating artistic production with God's life-giving power of creation. At different times and places in history, this has been interpreted as a ban on all reproductions of living things, and it is almost unheard of to find animals or humans depicted within a religious environment or in Quran manuscripts – designs based on geometry or stylized representations of vegetal forms were used instead.

THE ARABESQUE

Stylized foliate scrollwork is a recurrent motif in Islamic art, and has sometimes been named 'the arabesque'. In essence, this is a form of leafy palmette-leaf scrollwork, composed of tightly packed S-shaped tendrils. The inspiration seems to have come from the bands of vine and acanthus decoration popular in the classical world. Early hints of this influence were apparent in the 8th century, in the stonework decoration of the Umayyad palace of Mshatta in Jordan.

Over the centuries designers adjusted the style of this pattern, and created leafy scrolls which were ever more dense and intricate. With ever-increasing stylization, the leafy scrolls became less and less naturalistic. The popularity of this floral ornament was based on its infinite

Above A fine example of 16th-century Iznik tilework, from the Circumcision Chamber in Topkapi Palace, Istanbul, includes birds, peonies and lotus flowers.

Above Flowers were popular motifs, such as the one on an Iznik tile from the Selimiye Mosque, built under Selim II (1566–74) in Edirne (Turkey).

versatility: undulating floral scrolls could be adapted in size and made to fit monumental architectural spaces on tiled or painted surfaces, or reduced to fit the margins of manuscripts, or the decoration of metalwork and ceramic objects.

CHINESE MOTIFS

Islamic craftsmen borrowed a range of Chinese imagery following the Mongol invasions during the 13th century, when large quantities of blue and white porcelain, silk textiles and other goods were imported. The most common motifs were floral: large peonies and lotus blossoms were especially prominent, and were soon adopted into the design repertoire for manuscript illumination, ceramics and glass. Fabulous creatures from Chinese mythology also made an impact, and wiry stylized dragons began to appear in Islamic art, as did the Chinese phoenix.

In Chinese contexts the phoenix and the dragon had imperial connotations and the lotus was associated with the Buddha, but when incorporated into Islamic designs these motifs became purely decorative and lost their original meaning.

The cloud band or cloud scroll was another Chinese import; very stylized ribbon-like clouds were used as space-fillers in the same way as the arabesque. A good example of these is to be found on the monumental tile panels now attached to the exterior walls of the Circumcision Chamber in the Topkapi palace in Istanbul. The contrasting blue and white palette of these tiles was also copied from Chinese porcelain.

DECORATIVE OBJECTS

UNDER THE PATRONAGE OF THE MUGHALS, THE DECORATIVE ARTS REACHED UNPRECEDENTED HEIGHTS. ARTICLES OF EVERYDAY USE, SUCH AS INKWELLS, WERE OBJECTS OF OPULENCE AND BEAUTY.

Influenced by the arts of the wider Islamic world, yet firmly rooted in Indian traditions, Mughal style permeated every element of the Mughal courts. In the vast network of *karkhanas*, or imperial workshops, expert artists, artisans and craftsmen produced luxurious furnishings and objects for the Mughal palaces. Even practical objects, such as *huqqas* (water pipes), ewers and back scratchers, were fashioned from costly materials, such as jade and rock crystal.

The decorative themes echoed those found in architecture. Under Jahangir (reigned 1605–27), images of plants, animals and people appeared in a naturalistic style, and in Shah Jahan's reign (1628–58), floral plant motifs were popular.

JADE

The Mughal emperors of India were passionate admirers of jade. This passion is evident in the artistic innovation and outstanding technical virtuosity of jade objects produced in the court ateliers. Jade was the favourite hardstone for decorative objects including eating and drinking vessels, fittings for a variety of weapons and also personal artefacts such as pendants, mirror backs and inkpots.

For the Mughal emperors, jade formed a powerful link with their Timurid ancestors, whose jade carving traditions and objects formed the foundation for a distinctive Indo-Persian style.

One of the most exquisite pieces to survive is Shah Jahan's wine cup, dated to 1657. Made of pearly white jade, the cup is of a lobed half-gourd shape, tapering into a curving handle in the shape of the head of an ibex. The base is shaped like open lotus petals with radiating leaves. Other more utilitarian objects were also carved from jade. *Huqqa* bases that were filled with water to cool and purify

Above *The interlocking panels of this vaulted ceiling in the tomb of Itimad-al-Daulah contain different painted floral motifs.*

the smoke before it passed through the pipe are known, and also dagger handles, often in the form of horse's heads. These were presented as gifts by the ruler and worn on ceremonial occasions.

STONE INLAY

Mughal craftsmen were masters of the art of stone inlay, using a technique known as *parchin kari* in India, but also as *pietra dura* from the Italian tradition. Colourful semi-precious stones, such as lapis lazuli, carnelian and agate were inlaid into white marble, creating elaborate floral and geometric designs.

The tomb of Itimad al-Dawla in Agra was the first Mughal building to use this technique for its decoration which was also used to great effect in the Taj Mahal and the Red Fort in Delhi.

Left *A magnificent wine cup made of milky white jade and belonging to the Mughal ruler, Shah Jahan, dated 1657.*

Right The ancient art of bidri has survived for some 4,000 years. These huqqa *bowls were made in Hyderabad, a centre for bidri manufacture today.*

BIDRIWARE

Bidri is a technique known only in the Indian subcontinent, and takes its name from the city of Bidar, in the present-day state of Karnataka. Its origins are obscure, but the earliest surviving pieces date from the late 16th and early 17th centuries.

Bidri objects are cast from an alloy in which zinc predominates, though small amounts of lead, copper and tin may also be found. The decoration is inlaid with silver, or a combination of silver and brass. The final stage of the bidri process is to apply a saline mud paste over the entire surface which changes the dull grey of the alloy to a dense black colour. The shiny silver and brass inlays contrast very effectively with the matt black background.

ROCK CRYSTAL AND GLASS

The clear, ice-like appearance of rock crystal had a great appeal for the Mughals. Examples of rock crystal inlaid with precious gems survive from the mid-17th century, although the techniques of the inlay process were already known during Akbar's reign. Vessels, such as cups and bowls, were deeply engraved with floral patterns, others were inlaid with gold and set with precious stones.

Glass decanters with long necks had been produced in India for some time, but there is no hard evidence of glass production on a large scale until the Mughal period. Manuscript paintings show bottles of every shape and size arranged in wall niches or placed on the floor beside the emperor.

Right This Mughal wine cup, *made of emerald, gold and enamel, was recently sold at auction for £1.8 million, the highest price ever realized for a wine cup.*

THE LIVING IMAGE

FIGURAL REPRESENTATION WAS FREQUENTLY USED IN THE LUXURY ARTS OF THE ISLAMIC WORLD, THOUGH ORTHODOX DISAPPROVAL OF IMAGERY AFFECTED ART PRODUCED FOR SACRED USAGE.

Above A portrait of the physician and author Dioscorides appears in this 1229 Arabic translation of Dioscorides' De Materia Medica.

It is often believed that figural images are prohibited in Islamic art, but this is not the case. The Quran forbids the use of idols for religious worship. It does not ban figural representation. However, statements in *hadith* literature do speak out against the depiction of living creatures, and condemn the artist for seeming to create a living form, a power exclusive to God. For both of these reasons, images are never used in the Quran, mosque decoration or any strictly religious context in Islamic art. Instead, sacred books, objects and architecture are decorated with geometric designs, scrolling stylized leaves and flowers, and calligraphy – usually quoting Quranic verses.

FIGURATIVE ART

Outside of the sacred realm, pictures of people, animals and birds have been produced throughout Islamic art history, from Spain to India, in almost every decorative medium. Even three-dimensional sculpture was known: incense-burners, ewers, fountainheads and other figurines in the shape of animals and birds, as well as high-relief stucco wall panels. Particularly popular in the 11th–14th centuries, human and animal figures are the main decorative theme of rock crystal and ivories from Cairo, lustre and *minai* ceramics from Kashan, and inlaid metalwork from Mosul, to name only a few centres of production.

Right The surface of this 12th–13th-century Spanish bronze lion fountainhead is engraved with inscriptions expressing good wishes to the owner.

THEMES AND MOTIFS

Typical subjects dwell on aspects of court life: drinking with musical entertainment and dancers, romantic encounters, hunting on horseback, and formal throne scenes, where visiting dignitaries are received. Motifs of hunting animal pairs, such as a lion or hawk attacking a deer, were also commonly used. They reinforce the theme of power, and the ruler's right to it.

Many figural themes show artistic continuity from pre-Islamic times: Samanid polychrome ceramics made in the 10th century in north-eastern Iran seem to favour royal images recalling the pre-Islamic Sasanian empire of

Iran. In 10th–12th-century Egypt, Fatimid art shows a vogue for genre scenes, such as wrestlers, which may refer to inherited, classical and coptic traditions.

MANUSCRIPT PAINTING

Across the Islamic world, figures were illustrated in luxury manuscripts. Books have long been treasured in the Middle East, and many bibliophile rulers and the elite collected books with passion. Historic libraries

are recorded having thousands of volumes, and royal and private collectors often made their collections available to visiting scholars.

These were works of science as well as fine literature: the earliest surviving manuscript paintings from the Islamic period are geographical maps, diagrams of the constellations, plants, animals and even mechanical automata. Scientific illustration also extends to scenes of doctors and scholars at work: harvesting medicinal plants, treating a patient or consulting with other sages. The frontispiece portrait usually depicts the author in the company of his patron, whose support is thus acknowledged. This relates to the late classical genre of author portraiture, carried over into the Islamic world. The author's portrait was gradually replaced by that of his patron.

Above This 1330 illustration from the Shahnama *(Book of Kings) by Firdawsi shows a king and his court.*

LITERARY PORTRAITS

As long as their patrons could afford the expense, works of literature written in Arabic, Persian and, later, Turkish were also furnished with paintings: history, romantic poetry and heroic epics all provided dramatic subjects for illustration. Luxury copies of the classic Persian works by Firdawsi, Nizami and Saadi were made for rulers and the rich over the centuries, and Persian manuscript painting was produced to an exquisite level. The patron's portrait in the frontispiece remained a standard part of the book, and often provided an insight into the court world, showing princes, guests and entertainers, the architectural setting, furniture and tableware.

Above This 17th-century Isfahan copy of a 10th-century treatise on the stars discusses the constellation Bootes.

THE PRINCELY CYCLE

THE MOST FREQUENT FIGURAL SUBJECT IN ISLAMIC ART IS A THEMATIC RANGE REFERRED TO AS THE 'PRINCELY CYCLE', DESCRIBING THE PLEASANT PURSUITS OF COURT LIFE.

The theme of the princely cycle can be found across the various media in Islamic art. Works of inlaid metal, painted ceramics and especially manuscript paintings dwell upon the portrayal of the ruler and his world. In order to show appropriate reverence to royal status, the prince is usually depicted slightly larger than his surrounding courtiers, attendants and guests.

BANQUETS

Images of feasting were adopted in the early Islamic period from the Sasanian tradition. The principal figure is the enthroned ruler who is shown seated cross-legged and holding a cup in one hand. He is accompanied by attendants, such as the *saqi* or cup-bearer and courtiers who fulfilled the role of the *nadim* or boon companion.

Male and female musicians formed the entertainment, performing with a range of instruments, such as the lute, tambourine, flute and harp; they sometimes accompany dancers holding trailing scarves, and even acrobats. Images of such courtly entertainment might be shown taking place in palace interiors or outside within pavilions set within royal gardens.

Such images decorate items of luxury tableware: metal ewers and basins inlaid with copper and silver and ceramic dishes painted with metallic lustre and overglaze colours in the minai technique. The image is most often found in Persian painting, in both historical and poetic manuscripts. Rulers and princes are shown seated on thrones within elaborately decorated and carpeted interiors, surrounded by companions and entertained by musicians and dancers. Often lines of servants bearing dishes of fruits and sweetmeats are also depicted.

HUNTING

The iconography of the ruler out hunting was also adopted from earlier Persian tradition. The ruler is shown on horseback, with a hawk or falcon perched on his wrist ready to be launched in pursuit of prey such as hares or smaller birds.

Above A court assembly is shown in this manuscript painting from a late 15th-century copy of the Shahnama *by Firdawsi.*

Sometimes the hunter is shown with a cheetah riding behind him. This feline could be taught to capture, but not to kill the prey, which conformed to religious requirements; a passage in the Quran proscribes the eating of game killed by animals.

The lion hunt, an image that recurred frequently on silver-gilt bowls of the Sasanian period, demonstrated the ultimate subservience of the lion and symbolized the power of the king

to overcome his opponents. This notion of prey subservient to its predator was also demonstrated in images of lions or hawks attacking deer.

ILLUSTRATING AUTHORITY

The royal audience was another important theme in the princely cycle. The ruler is shown seated on a high-backed throne, usually at the centre of the composition. The throne is often flanked by guards, and in some versions winged spirits hold a canopy over the ruler to signify honour. Ranks of courtiers observe the scene, while visitors kneel or bow at the throne.

Above A pair of 19th-century Iranian tiles depict two noblemen hunting, one with a falcon, the other with a bow and arrow.

Left A 12th-century stucco panel from Iran depicts a ruler being attended by servants, and is framed within a 12-pointed star.

Below This section of a carved ivory panel, made in Egypt or Syria in the 12th century, illustrates scenes from a hunt, one of the many pleasures of court life.

The whole composition is deliberately designed to affirm and idealize authority and power.

A variant of the throne scene was included in some luxury manuscripts as the frontispiece illustration. The ruler is shown sitting in majesty, receiving the book from the author. By crediting him as the all-important sponsor of the work in this way, the artist places the ruler at the forefront of a major intellectual endeavour, thus endowing him with academic glamour.

TRADE WITH EUROPE

EUROPEANS WERE IMPRESSED BY THE HIGH QUALITY OF MATERIAL GOODS FROM THE ISLAMIC WORLD. LUXURY ITEMS WERE BROUGHT TO EUROPE, WHERE THEY INFLUENCED LOCAL CRAFTSMEN.

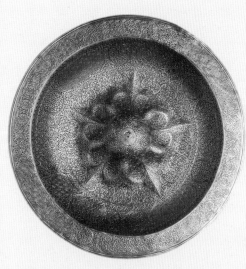

Across the Islamic world, a dedicated export market developed. Craftsmen in Egypt, Syria and al-Andalus worked to meet the demand from Europe. The luxury goods purchased by pilgrims and merchants included carpets, glass, ivories and textiles, as well as inlaid metalwork and ceramics.

VENICE AND THE MAMLUKS

The main European trading partners of Mamluk Egypt were Venice and Genoa. The great trade routes through Damascus and across the Red Sea to South and South-east Asia passed through Mamluk lands, and in many cities there was a permanent diplomatic staff from Venice, safeguarding the interests of Venetian merchants. Indeed, Francesco Foscari, Venice's longest-reigning doge (in power 1423–57), was born in Egypt. Venice was particularly important in the trade in glass and ceramics, but also played a key part in the import of metalwork. It is known from trade documents that Venetian merchants exported brass and copper in significant quantities to craftsmen in the Middle East and at the other end of the process imported the finished inlaid products.

At one time historians proposed that Muslim craftsmen actually lived and worked in Venice, producing what was once termed 'Veneto-Saracenic metalwork' for the local luxury market. Modern historians reject this theory, arguing that the crafts guilds in Venice were so tightly managed that no foreign workers would have been able to establish themselves in the city.

STATUS SYMBOLS

Items of inlaid metalwork imported from the Islamic world into Europe included ewers, incense-burners and candlesticks as well as basins. These acquisitions were then proudly and prominently displayed in the homes of the wealthy.

Above This fine engraved 16th-century brass dish with a raised centre may have been made in Italy in an Islamic style.

On many of these items, a space was left blank for a European coat of arms to be added by the customers.

Some of the artefacts, such as the Baptistère de St Louis (see opposite page), found their way into royal collections and from there into modern museums, where we can admire them today, and their provenance and history are carefully detailed. Another key area of evidence for the trade between the Islamic world and Europe can be found in Italian paintings of the Renaissance period. Islamic art objects were often depicted in portraits of patrons and their families, shown standing in a domestic context: many of the objects were beautiful, exotic and expensive – and so, naturally enough, they were symbols of status, wealth and international connections.

Above Danzig merchant George Gisze made a prominent display of his carpet, imported from what is now Turkey, when he was painted by Hans Holbein in 1532.

CERAMICS AND GLASSWARE

Imported wares were copied by local European craftsmen, and in some cases the trade in Islamic products inspired the development of European production centres. For example, craftsmen in the Middle East developed gilding and enamelling techniques for decorating glass. Afterward, in the 13th century, Venice became the European centre for decorated glass objects, in part because of its maritime trade with the Islamic world but also because exiled Byzantine craftsmen settled in Venice. The craftsmen in Venice used forms and decorative styles developed in the Islamic Middle East but also turned for inspiration to narratives and motifs from Italy's classical past.

Glazed lustre pottery from al-Andalus was also imported to Europe. In Italy, tin-glazed wares were named 'maiolica' after the contemporary Italian name for the island of Mallorca, which was a key staging post on the maritime route for pottery from al-Andalus. In Venice, Florence and elsewhere in Italy, craftsmen made their own maiolica wares from the late 1200s

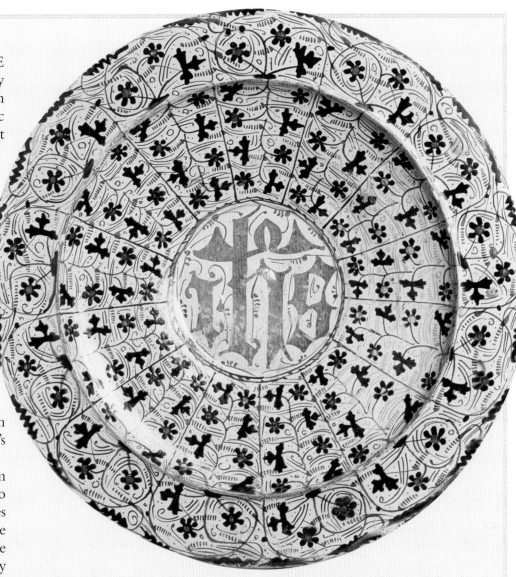

onward. From Middle Eastern potters, Italian craftsmen learned how to scrape through the glaze to uncover the darker surface beneath – a technique called 'sgraffiato'.

Above A Hispano-Moresque dish of tin-glazed maiolica, with the Christian monogram IHS in the centre. Stylized floral designs surround the central inscription.

Above The design on the Baptistère de St Louis shows dignitaries carrying weapons and symbols of their status at court.

THE BAPTISTÈRE DE ST LOUIS

A notable example of Mamluk export wares is the Baptistère de St Louis, an exquisite brass basin covered with figural engraved decoration and inlaid with silver and gold. The basin was signed by Muhammad ibn al-Zayn, probably in the mid-14th century – a time when this figural, decorative style had gone out of fashion among the Mamluk sultans and amirs, suggesting that the item was made for European customers.

The basin passed into the collection of the French royal family and was used as a vessel to hold holy water for the baptism of princes and princesses; it was part of the royal collection of the Sainte-Chapelle ('Holy Chapel') in the Château de Vincennes (built in the 14th century by King Charles V and now in the suburbs of Paris). The Baptistère de St Louis was given its name, which means the 'baptismal vessel of St Louis', because of an anachronistic association with St Louis (the French King Louis IX, died 1270). The basin is now in the Musée du Louvre in Paris.

GLASSMAKING

IN THE 9TH AND 10TH CENTURIES, ISLAMIC GLASSMAKERS DEVELOPED IMPRESSIVE NEW DECORATIVE TECHNIQUES FOR CUTTING AND COLOURING THE GLASS SURFACE.

Above This cup was found in a palace of the Abbasid Caliph al-Mutasim (reigned 833–42). Vertical lines of inscription read 'drink and be filled with delight' and 'made in Damascus'.

Long before the Arab conquest, glassmaking had flourished across the Middle East for more than two millennia. Glassmaking was a conservative craft in which technical methods continued unchanged over long periods. The political upheavals of the Islamic conquest had little impact on the glass workers, except that they increased the production of their wares in response to demand from their new patrons.

AN EXPORTED WARE
Islamic glass was traded widely across the Islamic world and also in Europe, China and South-east Asia. It was exported in the form of luxury vessels but also as broken glass, known as cullet, which was suitable for remelting and making new glass inexpensively. This wide distribution makes it difficult to identify with any certainty where much of Islamic glass was produced. One broad distinction is that glass workers in Iran and Iraq favoured cutting and moulding techniques, whereas those in Egypt and Syria preferred to experiment with colour.

LUSTRE GLASS
A technique known as lustre decoration was invented in the 7th century. This was a complex process where powdered metallic oxides containing silver or copper mixed with vinegar were painted on to a blown glass vessel, which was then reheated in a reducing kiln at a temperature lower than the original firing so that the vessel did not collapse. The oxides left a brownish or yellow stain, sometimes with a metallic sheen, on the pale glass. Several lustre-painted glasses have inscriptions, a few of them naming their patrons, making the value placed on such objects evident. Two lustre glasses have been found with inscriptions stating that they were made in Damascus.

PRODUCING CUT GLASS
The art of cutting glass became highly developed in Iran and Iraq in the 9th and 10th centuries. Glass vessels were blown into the desired shape and then allowed to cool to

Above This 16th-century manuscript painting shows the stages of glass-blowing and the tools required. On the right, a craftsman is blowing a glass bubble.

THE GLASSMAKING PROCESS
Glass is essentially made from silica, or sand, which melts at very high temperatures. To lower the melting point, a flux obtained from the ashes of the glasswort plant or from natron, a mineral widely available in Egypt and also used in the mummification process, was added to the silica and heated in an iron pot in the hottest part of the furnace. When the mixture had melted, the craftsman gathered up a mass, known as a 'gather', on the end of his blowpipe to create a bubble of glass, which he then shaped and decorated with various tools.

let the glass worker grind, cut and polish the surface on a rotating wheel – as he might do if working with gemstones. Facet cutting, a method that was popular in Iran in the Sasanian period (226–651 CE), was achieved by blowing vessels with relatively thick walls and then cutting away parts of the surface to create a honeycomb pattern of shallow facets. Fine geometric and floral patterns could be incised into the surface with a tool set with a diamond point, and this technique is referred to as scratch engraving. Several blue glass dishes of this type were found in the crypt of a temple in China that was sealed in 874.

The technique of relief-cut glass required extraordinary skill and precision. The pattern was created by cutting and grinding the surface to remove the background and most of the inner areas of the main design, leaving the outlines and some details in relief. A version

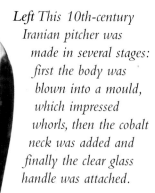

Left This 10th-century Iranian pitcher was made in several stages: first the body was blown into a mould, which impressed whorls, then the cobalt neck was added and finally the clear glass handle was attached.

of this technique is known as cameo glass: the colourless glass vessel was dipped in molten coloured glass to form a coating, and after cooling, sections of the coloured layer were cut away to form an overlaid decorative design.

TRAILED GLASS

In Syria and Egypt, a number of techniques were used where the glass was manipulated and decorated while it was hot and malleable. Applied trails of glass, in a contrasting colour to the vessel, could be wound around the vessel and then manipulated with a pointed tool or a fine pincer to create patterns in thin strands of glass. A group of small animal figures, shaped as camels or donkeys, have flasks (probably for storing perfume or scented oils) attached to their backs that are enclosed by a network of trailed threads like a basket. If the vessel with its applied trails was rolled on to a flat slab, known as a marver, the trails became integrated into the vessel wall and made striking wavy or festooned patterns; this is called 'marvered' glass.

Left To make this 10th–11th-century glass vessel, the clear glass matrix was dipped in a layer of molten turquoise glass; after it cooled, it was ground on a wheel using gem-cutting techniques.

ENAMELLED GLASSWARE

DURING THE 13TH AND 14TH CENTURIES, THE GLASSMAKERS OF SYRIA AND EGYPT PRODUCED ELABORATELY DECORATED GLASSWARE WITH ENAMEL AND GILDING.

Syrian and Egyptian glassmakers of this period were highly skilled. They produced glassware lavishly decorated with gilding and polychrome enamels, and their work was prized and widely exported within the Middle East and to Europe and China. One Egyptian author of the Mamluk period has written about richly ornamented glass that was produced in Damascus and being exported to Egypt, Syria, Iraq and Asia Minor. Crusaders to the Holy Land also referred to these wares in their chronicles and brought back many examples, which were donated to church treasuries or kept in their family collections.

EARLY ENAMELLING

The manufacture of enamelled glass was a lengthy and expensive process involving several stages. The first step was the creation of the glass object, which was free-blown or blown and shaped in a mould; the glass was then cooled slowly in an annealing oven. When the object was cold it was painted with enamel pigments and gold and reheated slowly until it could be picked up on a pontil (a tool used to hold the glass) and placed inside the mouth of the furnace to fuse the enamels to the vessel. Enamel colours and gold melt at different temperatures, so in theory they should have been applied and fired in sequence; however, this continual reheating would have risked the collapse of the object, and evidently methods were devised to fire all or most of the colours at once.

It is not clear exactly where or when the first experiments with enamelling took place, but a bottle inscribed with titles of the last Ayyubid ruler al-Malik al-Nasir (reigned 1237–60) has some tentative enamel decoration, though most of the surface was left undecorated.

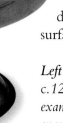

Left This bottle was produced in c.1237–60 and is the earliest datable example of Syrian or Egyptian enamelled glass.

Above This mid-13th-century beaker, decorated with polo players, was found beneath the altar of the church of Santa Margherita in Orvieto, Italy.

SKILLED ARTISANS

By the second half of the 13th century, the craftsmen had fully mastered the enamelling technique and began to use the glass almost like a canvas, painting it with all types of figurative scenes of courtly life in a variety of colours. Images of drinkers, musicians and polo players are painted in bands around bottles and bowls of many different shapes and sizes. Christian imagery was often integrated into the scheme, possibly because pilgrims and crusaders commissioned the vessels. For instance, a pilgrim flask in St Stephen's Cathedral in Vienna, Austria, was allegedly brought there filled with earth from Bethlehem. The neck is decorated with a band of figures, cowled and dressed like monks, the shoulders with falconers in roundels and the front with a troupe of musicians flanking a stylized cypress tree.

The patronage provided by the Mamluk court in the 14th century encouraged the expansion of the glassware industry. Glass workers demonstrated their virtuosity by creating large vessels in shapes and with geometric decorative schemes often inspired by contemporary metal and pottery prototypes. The decorative repertoire began to shift from an emphasis on the figural to a style dominated by epigraphic and floral designs, with motifs inspired by imported Chinese wares, such as the lotus flower.

MOSQUE LAMPS

Cairo in the 14th century was in the middle of a building boom triggered by the Mamluk caliphs and their amirs, who were eager to demonstrate their religious fervour by commissioning new mosques and *madrasas* (religious colleges). To light the interiors of these buildings, hundreds of highly decorated, enamelled-glass mosque lamps were made to be suspended from the ceilings. The jewelled colours of red, blue, green, yellow and white enamel with large areas of gilding must have glowed richly.

The decoration of these lamps consists of large areas of calligraphy and bands of intricate floral pattern. The inscription is often a specific and apposite verse from the Quran: 'God is the light of the heavens and the earth; His light is like a niche that contains a lamp, the light within like a glittering star.'

The patron of the lamp is generally identified in calligraphy and with a blazon containing the attribute marking the rank of the official.

Left The shape of this late 13th–14th-century bottle was modelled on the leather water flasks that pilgrims attached to their saddles.

Above This mid-14th-century Egyptian mosque lamp bears the titles and blazon of Amir Sayf al-Din Shaykhu, who rose to be commander in chief under the Mamluk Sultan, Hasan.

THE END OF AN INDUSTRY

The production of enamelled glass in Syria and Egypt began to decline in the late 14th century, and by the 15th century many workshops had closed altogether. When Timur sacked Damascus in 1400, it has been said that he removed its glass workers to his capital in Samarkand – however, there is no evidence of glass production from there. By the late 15th century, the production of enamelled glassware had shifted to Europe – to Venice, Italy, in particular.

POTTERY AND LUSTREWARE

IN AN ATTEMPT TO IMITATE IMPORTED CHINESE WARES, ISLAMIC POTTERS DEVELOPED A WHITE TIN GLAZE BUT SOON ADDED THEIR OWN DESIGNS WITH COBALT AND LUSTRE.

The earliest pottery production in the Islamic world was a continuation of local traditions. Functional green- and turquoise-glazed earthenwares were made for the storage and transportation of goods, such as oil, dates and honey. However, in the late 8th to early 9th centuries, the pottery industry in Iraq was transformed, and the first distinctively Islamic ceramics were produced here. This was a development that coincided with the luxurious taste and demands of the Abbasid court, and it was triggered by the importation of porcelain and stoneware items from China. These wares provided inspiration to the Iraqi potters, who sought to imitate them.

FOREIGN INFLUENCES
Basra was the main centre of pottery production: several contemporary writers describe the fine quality of the white clay found in deposits near the city and it was also the port of entry for imported Chinese wares that came by sea. Persian and Arab sailors had recently opened a direct sea route between the Persian Gulf and the South China Sea. They took ivory, incense, spices and pearls to China and returned with silk, paper and ceramics. The goods also travelled by land over the Silk Route. A contemporary account of one diplomatic gift to Harun al-Rashid, the caliph in Baghdad, included: '200 pieces of imperial porcelain, including basins and bowls and other things the like of which had never been seen before at a royal court, and 2,000 other

Chinese ceramic vessels, including covered dishes, large bowls and large and small pottery jars.'

BLUE-AND-WHITE POTTERY
The Iraqi potters could not reproduce the shiny white surface and hard compact body of the Chinese wares exactly because they did not have access to the same type of clay – white kaolin – or the kiln technology that was needed to achieve high firing temperatures. Instead, they closely imitated the Chinese vessel shapes and copied the whiteness of the surface by covering the yellow body of the pots with an opaque white glaze made by mixing tin oxide with a lead glaze.

Initially, the potters left the surfaces of these wares unadorned, like the Chinese prototypes, but it was not long before they began to add decoration in cobalt blue pigment. The colour had a tendency to sink into the glaze, an effect that has been described as 'ink on snow'. The designs were generally limited to floral and geometric motifs or calligraphic inscriptions. The use of writing, in the form of signatures and phrases, such as 'blessing to its owner', was an entirely new and Islamic decorative device. In a second phase, splashes of green were added to the cobalt designs, probably influenced by imported Chinese splashware vessels.

Above Iraqi potters imitated Chinese white wares by coating the earthenware body with an opaque white glaze, as seen in this 9th-century bowl.

LUSTRE GLAZING
Following the commercial success of the blue-and-white pottery, the Basra potters developed a new technique known as lustre glazing, a complex process that required expensive materials. Borrowed from

Above This 9th-century dish has been pressed into a mould to form the relief decoration. The raised dots and lustre glaze were used to imitate metal.

glass technology, the technique used powdered metallic oxides of silver and copper, which when applied to the ceramic body produced a lustrous metallic sheen. The pots were painted with a plain white glaze and fired in an ordinary kiln. When they were cool, the potter painted on the design in a mix of metallic compounds that were finely ground together, mixed with clay and diluted in grape juice or vinegar. The vessel was then put into a reduction kiln and fired a second time; carbon monoxide in the reducing atmosphere extracted the oxygen from the silver and copper oxides and bonded them as a thin layer of metal on to the surface of the glaze.

STYLISTIC CHANGES

The earliest lustre-glazed vessels were decorated with a range of tones known as polychrome lustre and were characterized by busy geometric and floral patterns that entirely covered the surface. Over time the process was simplified and a single golden colour, described as monochrome lustre, was adopted. This simplification may have been intended to reduce the costs of the process, or it could have been that after much experimentation the potters had achieved a real understanding and control of the technique.

With the change in palette, a new iconography was developed and the abstract patterning was replaced with figural imagery. Large-scale figures of men bearing arms, or seated and holding a glass, or animals, such as deer, camels and birds, became popular. These monochrome lustreware pieces are particularly distinctive; the contours of the image are outlined, leaving a narrow white space to separate

Above *This late 9th–early 10th-century bowl is painted with a stylized figure in a cross-legged position. It resembles a bodhisattva, which is a Buddhist religious figure.*

and distinguish it from the background, which is filled with roughly shaped dots or dashes like the punching found on metalwork. In this period, the Abbasid rulers recruited their armies from the tribes of Central Asia and it was probably through these Turkish immigrants that this type of imagery was introduced.

By the late 10th century, pottery production in Basra declined. Many of the potters seem to have moved to Egypt, where the Fatimid court was beginning to flourish.

Above *By the late 9th–early 10th century, potters in Iraq were expertly using lustre and had limited the palette to one colour.*

SAMANID POTTERY

NISHAPUR AND SAMARKAND WERE MAJOR POTTERY CENTRES IN THE 10TH CENTURY, PRODUCING WHITE SLIPWARES WITH CALLIGRAPHIC DESIGNS AND POLYCHROME WARES WITH FIGURAL DECORATION.

Excavations made in the cities of Nishapur and Samarkand have uncovered kilns along with other evidence of pottery production. Samanid pottery was made using slip technology, where a fine clay diluted with water, known as 'slip', was poured over the earthenware body of the vessel to form a smooth, even layer. When dry, the surface was decorated with more slip that had been coloured by adding different oxides to the mixture. Finally, a transparent lead glaze was applied over the ware, which was used to seal in the slip colours and intensify their hue.

EPIGRAPHIC STYLE

Some of the most impressive examples of Islamic ceramics were made during this period in both Samarkand and Nishapur. Using a variety of different styles of *kufic* calligraphy, the potters inscribed various aphorisms, or proverbs, around the walls of large flat dishes or deep bowls. Wares decorated in this fashion are known as epigraphic pottery. Sometimes the letters were stretched and elaborately decorated with knots and foliated terminals in order to fit the proportions of the vessel. The background colour was generally white and the calligraphy was usually applied in a dark brownish black, sometimes with

Right The kufic *inscription on this large, 10th–11th century earthenware dish reads: 'The taste of science is bitter at first but sweeter than honey in the end.'*

accents appearing in tomato red. However, in a few examples this palette is reversed, so that white calligraphy stands out from a dark background. Occasional birds, drawn with spare, bold lines and sometimes enclosing the word *baraka*, meaning 'blessing', are the only variants found in these wares.

POLYCHROMATIC WARES

In complete contrast to the monochromatic palette that was used for producing epigraphic ware, a colourful and highly patterned polychromatic ware seems to have been the speciality of Nishapur. On these bowls, a vivid yellow colour serves as a background to a riot of human figures, animals, birds and floral motifs arranged in hectic rotating patterns, which were coloured in green, dark brown and with touches of brick red. The wide range of decorative themes was

Above Over time the epigraphic style used in Nishapur and Samarkand evolved and red was added to enhance the monochromatic palette. This late 10th–11th-century bowl is decorated with dark brown and red slips.

probably drawn from local myths and folklore: many of the figures wear Persian costume and hold objects that have been associated with Zoroastrian ritual. Other pieces have explicitly Christian motifs, such as Nestorian crosses.

ESTABLISHING DATES

Unfortunately, the archaeologists at Nishapur could not establish a clear chronology for these two contrasting types of pottery. However, Richard Bulliet (b.1940), an American historian who specializes in medieval Islamic history, looked at the dated coins and types of ceramic excavated with them at three sites and deduced that more epigraphic pottery was found in the earlier sites and more figural ware in the later sites. He extrapolated from this distribution that the epigraphic ware appealed to the earliest settlers and converts who read Arabic and wanted to uphold

the traditions of the Abbasid court, whereas the colourful, figurative ware appealed to the indigenous population who were trying to maintain their Persian traditions. Bulliet even suggested that the different shapes of each type of ware represented the different dietary traditions of these two groups: the large flat dishes and bowls with calligraphic decoration were perfect for serving typically Arab dishes of rice and grilled meat, while the rounded bowls of the figurative ware were better suited to the more liquid Persian dishes.

FOREIGN INFLUENCES

The excavations at Nishapur also uncovered large numbers of imported Iraqi wares, such as lustreware pieces and blue-and-white ware with green splashes. The potters of Nishapur had tried to imitate both types, but it is clear they did not have access to the necessary ingredients or the specialized knowledge and were forced to approximate the techniques with locally available materials. They used a yellow-green slip and a glossy transparent glaze to imitate the colour and sheen of lustreware and copied the distinctive style of decoration closely. The same was the case with the blue-and-white

Above The swirling leaf scroll on this 10th–11th-century shallow bowl replaces the more usual band of calligraphy. It was painted in manganese slip.

Below This Nishapuri 10th–11th-century bowl shows a figure on a horse with a cheetah on its rump. Birds, rosettes and calligraphic elements are scattered around the background.

wares; Nishapuri potters do not seem to have had access to cobalt so substituted manganese, which produced a dark purplish colour, but combined with green splashes it produced a fair imitation.

Another popular type of ware excavated in Nishapur, but with a wide distribution across the Middle East and probably made in many centres, was splashed ware. It was made with either a plain surface or with an incised design that is sometimes described as 'sgraffiato' (Italian for 'scratched'). Such pieces were covered with white slip, and then metallic oxides were used to produce various colours: copper for vivid green, iron for yellow-brown and manganese for purple were splashed on to the surface in stripes or spots. One of the few datable vessels is a jar from Susa, which contained a hoard of coins, the latest one dated 955–56.

KASHAN POTTERY

CERAMIC PRODUCTION FLOURISHED DURING THE LATE 12TH CENTURY IN KASHAN, WHERE NEW MATERIALS AND TECHNIQUES WERE USED TO MAKE WARES WITH ELABORATE DESIGNS.

In the 12th century, an important new ceramic production centre was established at Kashan in central Iran. There are no records of the city's industrial history before this time, but it was located close to the sources of raw ingredients and fuel needed to produce luxury pottery. The Persian words for tiles and pottery are *kashi* or *kashani*; it seems their manufacture became so closely identified with the town that the product came to be named after it.

Below This early 13th-century stool or low table is made from stonepaste with a white glaze and lustre decoration; the six sides are identically decorated.

A NEW BODY MATERIAL

Much is known about the technical aspects of pottery production in this period. A treatise written by Abu'l Qasim al-Tahir in 1301 included a section on the art of glazed ceramics. He was well-qualified to write this manual since four generations of his family worked as potters in Kashan.

One of the triggers for this new production was the development of a new body material known as stonepaste (or fritware), which was white and could be made to appear translucent – both highly regarded qualities of Chinese porcelain. The technology for this new body was

Above The composition of this 1210 Kashan stonepaste dish, with a sleeping boy beside a pond with a naked figure, along with a horse and attendants, has been interpreted as a mystical allegory regarding the quest for the Divine.

probably introduced to Kashan by potters from Egypt, who had moved east in search of new patronage after the collapse of the Fatimid regime. The recipe for the stonepaste body is given by Abu'l Qasim. He lists its ingredients as ten parts of sugar stone (or quartz), crushed and then strained through coarse silk, one part crushed glass and one part fine white clay.

Initially, the potters exploited the whiteness of this new body and made finely potted, thin-walled vessels that were simply covered in a transparent alkaline glaze. The walls were moulded in relief, and holes pierced through the pattern would become filled with glaze, producing a translucent effect. The stonepaste body was an excellent surface for decoration and it was not long before coloured glazes, particularly brilliant shades of cobalt and turquoise, were added.

THE KASHAN STYLE

A technical manual written in 1196 by Muhammad al-Jawhar al-Nishapuri devotes a chapter to the ingredients and processes involved

the vessel and then carved parts away, leaving the design behind in silhouette. Later experimentation revealed that the black pigment could be painted directly on to the surface of the vessel; this discovery allowed the potters greater freedom and fluency in their designs and the earlier clumsily carved decoration was abandoned in favour of quite delicately scrolled floral designs and bands of elegant cursive inscription. Details in cobalt were sometimes added, but this was much less stable and often ran under the glaze.

END OF AN ERA
Kashan was attacked by the Mongols in the 1220s, and although ceramic production suffered, it was not destroyed; lustre production was curtailed and for a time pieces were not signed or dated until production was revived in the Ilkhanid period.

Above This Kashan stonepaste bowl with minai *decoration is from c.1300. It shows a scene from the* Shahnama, *in which the hero Faridun rides the cow Barmaya and leads the captive Zahhak.*

in overglaze *minai* (from the Arabic for 'enamel') decoration, and lustre decoration, in which metallic oxides were painted over the glaze and fixed in a second reduction firing to create a lustre, or metallic, sheen. The Kashan potters became renowned for these two techniques.

Minai ware used a new polychrome technique developed so that the figurative imagery could be rendered with greater clarity. Like lustre decoration, this was an expensive process that required several firings in the kiln. Areas of the design were painted with colours such as turquoise, cobalt, grey and purple on to the white glaze and the piece was fired.

Further details were then applied in black, red and gold before a second firing. The figurative decoration probably reflects designs found on contemporary illustrated manuscripts and wall paintings, although none of these survive.

By 1200, what is known as the 'Kashan' style was fully developed and the majority of dated objects and tiles are decorated in this way.

UNDERGLAZE PAINTING
Another Kashan innovation was the development of underglaze painting. In the first stages of this technique, the potters applied a layer of black slip (a liquid clay) to

Right This early 13th-century stonepaste jug with black painted decoration under a turquoise glaze has a cockerel-shaped head. The outer body is pierced using a technique borrowed from metalwork; a hidden inner body contained the liquid.

ILKHANID POTTERY

BY THE MID-13TH CENTURY, CHINESE MOTIFS WERE APPEARING ON ILKHANID CERAMICS, REFLECTING A CHANGE OF DECORATIVE STYLE THAT WAS INFLUENCED BY THE MONGOL INVASIONS.

During the Mongol invasions in the first half of the 13th century, the production of luxury ceramics at Kashan was severely disrupted. Large-scale production was not resumed until the 1260s, by which time the Mongols had installed themselves as the Ilkhanid rulers of Iran and had established their capital in Tabriz.

There seems little doubt that ceramic workshops would have been active in the capital, and Abu'l Qasim, a contemporary historian and member of the famous Kashani family of potters, refers in his treatise to the type of wood burnt to fire the kilns in Tabriz. So far it has not proved possible to identify what type of wares were made there. However, it is known that the Abu Tahir family of potters remained closely involved in the running of the pottery workshops in Kashan in Iran, because tiles signed by them have survived.

MONGOL INFLUENCES

Ilkhanid pottery shows a distinct change of style in its decoration, which must have reflected the tastes of the new patrons. The so-called Pax Mongolica, or 'Mongol Peace', created an environment of free

Above The Ilkhanids were passionate about hunting. Birds and animals of the chase, such as these startled hares, were popular decorative themes.

cultural exchange across the Islamic world and beyond, and many Chinese motifs were introduced into the Islamic artistic vocabulary. New ornamental motifs included lotuses and peonies, cloud bands, dragons and phoenixes. The new styles also show the influence of Chinese design in vessel shape. Celadon forms, such as the rounded bowl with relief petals on the exterior, known as the lotus bowl, were widely imitated.

Lustreware was still being produced with a different emphasis. Floral and geometric designs replaced the earlier figurative schemes, and turquoise as well as cobalt formed a counterpoint to the lustre. The principle of the overglaze *minai*, or enamelled, technique was not abandoned, but the palette was transformed by 1301, when Abu'l Qasim says that the old style was replaced by *lajvardina*. The word *lajvard* is Persian for 'lapis lazuli', which describes the colour of the cobalt background

Left An Ilkhanid stonepaste tile with cobalt glaze and overglaze decoration of white, red and gold.

over which was painted a showy combination of white and gold, with gold leaf applied in intricate, often geometric designs.

SULTANABAD WARE

A new style of wares became known as Sultanabad ware, not because they were produced in the city, but many pieces were found near it. With a new monochromatic palette, probably inspired by Cizhou wares imported from China, the body of the vessels was covered with a thin slip (liquid clay) of a purplish grey or pale brown colour on which designs were painted in a thick white slip, outlined in black and set against a black hatched ground. A loose overall pattern of leaves painted in the thick white slip forms the background to the main motif, which often has a Mongol flavour: pheasants, ducks in flight, deer and gazelles, and scenes of figures in Mongol dress.

ARCHITECTURAL TILES

The use of tiles to decorate architectural surfaces was an old tradition in Iran, but it had a new resurgence in the Ilkhanid period. The potters concentrated on fulfilling commissions for producing tiles for shrines, mosques and palaces. A number of tombs commemorating Shiah and Sufi saints were built in the late 13th and 14th centuries with whole walls decorated with eight-pointed and cross-shaped lustre tiles.

Takht-i Sulayman, the summer palace built by the Mongol ruler Abaqa Khan c.1275, consisted of several buildings that were lavishly decorated with tiles. Many fragments were discovered on the site and tiles are thought to have been used to line both internal and external walls. The tiles were of all different shapes and sizes, from large rectangular figural scenes to smaller geometric shapes that would have formed part of interlocking patterns. The production techniques also showed a wide range: lustre, *lajvardina*, monochrome glazed, underglazed and unglazed tiles were found together. A kiln and workshop were also discovered, indicating that the workload was so extensive that craftsmen were transferred to work on the site. Some of the tiles were painted with episodes from the *Shahnama* (Book of Kings), while others were inscribed with quotations from this same epic history, and further tiles show the dragon and phoenix, mythical animals that were Chinese royal symbols. By invoking both Persian and Chinese symbols of authority, the Ilkhanid rulers were clearly underlining their own legitimacy.

Right *Walls were often tiled with geometric patterns of eight-pointed star tiles with cross-shaped tiles filling the interstices.*

CERAMICS OF SAFAVID IRAN

IMPORTED CHINESE POTTERY INFLUENCED THE PRODUCTION OF TIMURID POTTERY IN THE 15TH CENTURY. THE SAFAVIDS FOLLOWED THE TIMURID TRADITIONS IN THE 16TH AND 17TH CENTURIES.

From the 9th century onward, Chinese porcelain was highly valued in the Middle East and was almost continuously imported by land and sea. Blue-and-white wares were made specifically for export at the Jianxi kilns of Jingdezhen in China, and were imported into Syria and Egypt from the late 14th century.

Although imported Chinese porcelain was used as tableware, it was also displayed in specially designed pavilions, known as *chini khaneh*. The Mughal Emperor Babur, who visited the collection of Ulugh Beg (d.1449), one of the amirs during the Timurid dynasty, described a hall lined with porcelain tiles ordered from China. The interior was probably lined with wooden panelling cut into niches of various shapes to house vessels of different forms. This type of display has been found illustrated in manuscript paintings of the Timurid and Safavid periods.

When the Turkic Amir Timur (reigned 1370–1405) conquered Damascus in 1400, he brought its craftsmen back to his capital Samarkand, where the conscripts began producing blue-and-white pottery using the manufacturing techniques they were familiar with. The stonepaste body was made using sand, which was at variance with the traditional Iranian practice of using river pebbles.

After Timur's death in 1405, the Timurid capital moved to Herat, and in 1411 conscripted workmen were allowed to travel home. This resulted in craftsmen settling in a number of areas. Three main pottery centres developed from the late Timurid era into the Safavid period at Nishapur, Mashhad and Tabriz.

Above This elegant vessel, with Chinese-inspired scenes, was used for smoking tobacco.

ARCHITECTURAL TILES

Timurid buildings were lavishly decorated with tiles. Tile-makers used a range of techniques: glazed bricks, carved and glazed terracotta, tile mosaic and *cuerda seca*, overglaze enamelled, underglaze painted, relief and occasionally lustre tiles.

Tile mosaic was made from slabs of glazed tile that were cut after firing into interlocking shapes. The individual pieces were put together face down on a drawing of the design and plaster was poured over the back and strengthened by canes; when dry, the panel was attached to the wall. This was a labour-intensive process, but a faster alternative, named the *cuerda seca* ('dry rope') technique, developed in Spain. This overcame the technical difficulties of firing several colours together by outlining each area with an oily substance, which burnt off during firing to leave an outline in relief.

When Shah Abbas I (reigned 1587–1629) moved his Safavid

Left In 1607–8, Shah Abbas I gave the palace collection of Chinese porcelain to his family shrine at Ardabil. Individual niches were built in the shrine to house the pieces.

capital to Isfahan in 1598, a great period of construction began. Palaces and other secular structures were decorated with square tiles individually painted in polychrome glazes. These tiles were then combined to form large pictorial scenes with elegant, languid figures arranged in garden settings in the new style developed by Reza Abbasi, chief painter of the court atelier.

SAFAVID BLUE AND WHITE

In 1607–8, Shah Abbas I donated the imperial collection of Chinese porcelain, some 1,162 mostly blue-and-white pieces, to his ancestral shrine at Ardabil in north-western Iran, where they were displayed in a specially renovated building. Inspired by this and the newly popular Wanli porcelain being imported from China, production of blue-and-white increased to satisfy the local demand.

The East India Company had built up a trading network in Iranian ports and when the fall of the Ming dynasty in 1644 disrupted Chinese exports, the Persian workshops became one of the biggest suppliers of blue-and-white to

Europe. Persian and European sources single out Kirman as the centre that was producing the finest blue-and-white wares. Mashhad was also an important centre and potters there revived the use of the lustre technique, producing vessels decorated with delicate landscape and floral designs.

KUBACHI WARE

The term 'Kubachi' ware has been used to describe pottery of both the Timurid and Safavid periods. The name refers to a village in the Caucasus, where 19th-century travellers discovered large quantities of ceramic dishes hanging on the walls of the houses. The dishes were in many different styles – blue-and-white, turquoise-and-black, and polychrome – but were identifiable by the holes drilled in the foot ring for hanging

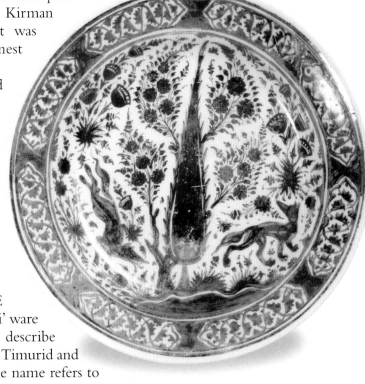

Above A 17th-century stonepaste dish with coppery lustre, probably from Mashhad, Iran. The design was inspired by marginal decoration on manuscripts.

and a crackling in the glaze. However, it became clear they were never made there and it has only recently been established that they were made in Nishapur, Mashhad, Tabriz and Isfahan.

Below Individually painted square tiles were often combined, as here, to form large pictorial scenes.

IZNIK POTTERY

THE SKILLED CRAFTSMEN OF IZNIK WERE RENOWNED FOR THEIR CERAMIC POTTERY AND TILES, AND THEIR PRODUCTION REACHED ITS PEAK DURING THE 16TH CENTURY.

The production of glazed earthenware at Iznik, formerly Nicaea, went back to the 13th century. In the 15th century, potters from Iran introduced the technology for making the hard white ceramic body known as stonepaste. The tile work of the mosque of Sultan Mehmet in Bursa, dated 1419–24, is signed by 'the masters of Tabriz' (a city in north-western Iran). The typical Iznik pottery body is hard and white, coated in a white slip (liquid clay) made of the same raw materials as the body but ground more finely. The transparent glaze is particularly brilliant and glossy.

EARLY PRODUCTION

The late 15th century was the beginning of large-scale production. The imperial workshops in Istanbul were responsible for many of the designs that were applied to the pottery vessels using stencils. Entire compositions or individual motifs were drawn on wax paper, the outlines were pricked and the design was laid over a tile or vessel and charcoal dust sprinkled though the holes. The first phase of design, inspired by both Chinese porcelain and the radial designs of Ottoman metalwork, consisted of tightly drawn arabesques reserved in white on dense, often

Above The walls of Rüstem Pasha Mosque are covered in tiles. Designs include a repetition of serrated saz leaves, Chinese-style cloud bands, plus tulips and carnations.

blackish cobalt ground. By the beginning of the 16th century, the blue had become paler, there was a greater use of white and the decoration had become looser.

TABRIZ INFLUENCE

In 1514, Sultan Selim I captured Tabriz and brought back 38 master craftsmen, including 2 tile cutters and at least 16 painters; one of these was Shahquli, who became head of the workshop in 1526 and initiated a new, more Persian style typified by the 'saz leaf and rosette' style, a harmonious combination of serrated leaves and large, many-petalled flowers.

One of the most impressive commissions of this period is a series of five massive tiles (each one

Left The floral spray on this late 16th-century dish includes tulip, rose and saz leaf – a classic combination. Red was applied thickly to survive the firing.

Right The distinctive pattern of tight foliated spirals on this mid-16th-century tondino – a small bowl with broad rim – was derived from manuscript illumination, particularly the tughra, *or imperial monogram.*

125cm/50in high), made for the walls of the Sunnet Odasi, or Circumcision Chamber, in the Topkapi Palace. These tiles were decorated with imaginary beasts grazing in a landscape of swirling leaves and flowers in various shades of blue and turquoise.

A new style was developed during the reign of Suleyman 'the Magnificent' (1520–66), in which the motifs were outlined in dark green or black for better definition, and new colours, such as purple and olive green, were introduced. A mosque lamp in this style is signed by its maker Musli.

ARCHITECTURAL TILES
Suleyman was a great patron of architecture, particularly religious buildings, and from 1550 tile making became the pre-eminent concern of the pottery workshops. The palette of soft colours used in vessel decoration needed to be altered, because when viewed from a distance these tones were muddy and indistinct. The colour red was introduced for better impact and visibility but had to be applied thickly to survive the firing. The red colouring was made from Armenian bole, a powerful astringent that the Ottomans used to heal circumcision wounds.

Sinan was made chief architect in 1538 and put in charge of all ceramics and architectural industries. He needed to have a close relationship with the Iznik potteries to ensure that the tiles were made to the correct dimensions to fit his building plans.

The new palette was so successful on tiles, it was eventually applied also to vessel production. The potters were inventive and developed many new shapes, some of which were based on metal and leather items, and many new designs. The floral style was still the most popular, particularly a spray of carnations, tulips and hyacinths springing from a central tuft, but there were also figural designs with animals and ships.

DECLINING INDUSTRY
In the 17th century, the industry started to decline. This was closely linked with the decline of Ottoman rule but also with the construction of the Sultan Ahmet Mosque, which while employing many tile makers during the peak of its ten-year construction period, eventually put them out of business. Sultan Ahmet was obsessed with tiles and ordered over 20,000 from Iznik. Extra clay had to be imported from Kutahya, and the tile makers were forbidden to do other work in the meantime. When work was completed, many potters must have gone bankrupt because they had been forced to neglect other production.

Right This 1549 mosque lamp is signed on the base by its maker, 'the poor and humble Musli', and the inscription around the base is dedicated to Esrefzade, a local saint of Iznik.

LUSTREWARE

SKILLED POTTERS MIGRATED FROM BASRA TO SEEK THE PATRONAGE OF THE FATIMIDS IN THEIR FLOURISHING CAPITAL, CAIRO. THE LUSTREWARE THEY PRODUCED WAS SUPERBLY PAINTED.

During the Abbasid Caliphate, Egypt was controlled by Ahmad ibn Tulun, a governor brought up in Samarra who surrounded himself with luxurious objects. Large quantities of lustreware items were imported from Basra, and when civil unrest disrupted that city in *c*.870, some of its artists skilled in the lustre technique may have migrated to ibn Tulun's rising artistic centre. (One source of evidence is from a condiment dish of this period now in the British Museum; it is signed by Abu Nasr of Basra in Misr, that is, in Egypt; however, the dish was not painted with a lustre glaze.)

When the Fatimids established their capital in Cairo a century later, they too attracted a wave of new craftsmen seeking the court's patronage. Among them were potters from Iraq, who brought with them the highly specialized knowledge needed for the manufacture of lustre pottery.

POTTERY BODY

The local supply of clay was not of the same high quality as was available around Basra, and Fatimid lustreware items are of much poorer quality. The potting body is often heavy, the glazes are technically imperfect and, overall, the pottery

Above The female figure portrayed on this shallow, early 11th-century lustre bowl has her foot raised as she dances. The dancer also holds castanets in her hands.

has a rougher, more careless finish. However, while the bodies and glaze may have been of inferior quality, any defects were amply compensated for by the superior quality of the painting.

Sometime in the early 11th century, probably in an effort to overcome the poor quality of the earthenware, potters started to experiment with a new body, which had quartz and glass added to the clay to make it harder, whiter and more like porcelain. The technology had a long history in Egypt, although it had lain dormant for a long time; in the Pharaonic period (278–330) a glassy, quartz-rich body known as faience had been developed.

A DEVELOPING STYLE

Initially, the potters worked in a recognizably 'Basra' style, using the same type of large abstracted figures set into a highly patterned

Left A leopard is shown with its keeper in this 11th-century lustre bowl. The figures were 'reserved', or unpainted, against the lustre background, and the details were highlighted with lustre.

lustreware and other pottery items in the Cairo markets. These were so highly prized in Italy they were often set into the walls of churches, a fashion particularly popular in Pisa, where several churches built at the beginning of the 12th century have Egyptian, as well as Syrian and North African bowls, known as *bacini*, cemented into their façades. Fragments of pottery from Syria and Egypt were also set into mosaics in several churches in and around Ravello, perhaps to make use of the glowing colours if the pieces had broken in transit.

In the late 11th century, there was economic and political unrest in Cairo and many of the potters left the area to seek patronage in safer areas such as Syria and Iran.

Left The gazelle on this early 11th-century lustre bowl was a popular motif in Fatimid decorative arts. It is also found on woodwork and ivory.

background. As the Egyptian potters became more confident, they began to paint a wide variety of scenes of courtly life in a realistic style: musicians and dancers, scenes of horsemen ready for hunting, exotic animals from the court menagerie, such as a giraffe led by its keeper. They also illustrated scenes from everyday life, such as cockfighting and wrestling. The market for this luxurious pottery was not confined to the court but also appealed to wealthy members of the wider society, which included merchants and minor officials.

AN EXPORTED COMMODITY
During the 11th century, Egypt dominated Mediterranean trade and developed close trade links with Italy, whose merchants travelled to Cairo and bought

SIGNED BY MUSLIM
The fragmentary rim of a dish in the Benaki Museum in Athens, Greece, contains the inscription: 'The work of Muslim ibn al Dahan (Muslim, son of the painter) to please Hasan Iqbal al-Hakimi.' The patron cannot be identified, but he must have been an official at the court of the Caliph al-Hakim (reigned 996–1021). More than 20 fragments and pieces with the signature of Muslim are known, sometimes (as with this dish) in an obvious place within the main decorative scheme and sometimes on the underside of the vessel. It is possible that the signature indicated the mark of the workshop rather than the potter. This suggestion is backed by the wide range of styles, from the floral and epigraphic to an elaborate figural piece, found in pieces signed Muslim.

Right This 11th-century bowl with a griffin set within a frame of floral design is signed by Muslim. As with the styles, the quality of the pieces with this signature was diverse.

SPANISH LUSTREWARE

THE SKILLED POTTERS OF ISLAMIC SPAIN CREATED MASTERPIECES IN CERAMICS, USING THE ISLAMIC TECHNIQUE OF LUSTRE PAINTING THAT ARRIVED IN SPAIN IN THE 11TH CENTURY.

It is thought that the technique of lustre decoration was invented in Iraq at the end of the 8th century by potters who borrowed techniques from glass technology. Powdered metallic compounds of copper and silver were painted on to the fired ceramic body, which was fired again at a low temperature in a kiln with a reduced oxygen supply. After cooling, the object was polished to reveal the lustrous metallic sheen.

Lustre-decorated ceramics were popular in Egypt during the Fatimid period from the late 10th century. The technique probably spread from Egypt to Spain in the early 11th century, where fragments of imported Fatimid lustreware pottery have been found. Fatimid potters may have moved west to the wealthy patrons of Islamic Spain, bringing the secrets of this complicated technique with them. The earliest lustreware made in Spain is a bowl that can be dated to the early 11th century. There is evidence for the dating of early Spanish lustreware in the so-called *bacini*, the imported glazed bowls that were used to decorate the façades of 12th-century churches in northern Italy, particularly Pisa. These show that the Spanish potters had mastered lustre production by the early 12th century.

EARLY SPANISH LUSTRE

By the 13th century, a lustreware industry was established in the port town of Málaga. The Arabic word *mālaqah* has been found written on a number of lustre fragments, indicating they were made in the town, which had grown in size and wealth under the patronage of the Nasrid rulers from 1238.

Early documentary evidence of Spanish lustreware is found in a document from Britain dated 1289, which mentions that pottery of 'a strange colour' was bought from a Spanish ship in Portsmouth for Queen Eleanor of Castile, who was the wife of King Edward I. In 1303, another document lists the customs duty that was paid on pottery from Málaga, which was described as '*terra de Malyk*', when it was imported into the town of Sandwich in Kent. The fact

Above This dish, made in the pottery-making centre of Manises, near Valencia, in 1496, bears the arms of Ferdinand of Aragon and Isabella of Castile.

that these ceramics were exported as far as Britain shows that lustreware was prized as a luxury object. The Moroccan traveller Ibn Battuta wrote in about 1350 that 'at Málaga is made the wonderful gilded pottery that is exported to the remotest countries.'

ALHAMBRA VASES

The magnificent 'Alhambra vases' have been described as the closest that pottery has ever come to architecture. Standing almost as tall as a human being, they are the largest Islamic ceramics ever made. Ten unique vases survive mostly intact, but excavated fragments suggest a greater production. The vases have been found in Spain, Sicily and Egypt, indicating that they were exported throughout the Mediterranean. Analysis of fragments of a vase found in Fustat, Egypt, confirmed that they were made in Málaga under the Nasrid Empire during the 14th century.

The name 'Alhambra vases' comes from the theory that they may have been made to grace the wall niches in the halls of the

Left This large Hispano-Moresque lustre dish, made from earthenware, dates from the 15th century.

Nasrid Alhambra Palace in Granada. Their distinctive, elegant shape resembles that of traditional unglazed storage jars known as *tinajas*, used to store and transport oil, wine and water. However, the vast size and winged handles of the Alhambra vases mean they could not have been easily lifted, while the rich decoration suggests a purely ornamental function.

The golden lustre and cobalt blue decorative scheme is usually arranged in horizontal bands that are decorated with arabesques, inscriptions and symbolic motifs, such as the *khamsa*, or 'hand of Fatima'. The monumental inscription on the vase in Palermo repeats continuously the word

Left One of the so-called 'Alhambra vases', this vessel stands over 1.2m (4ft) high and has golden lustre and cobalt blue decoration.

Above This earthenware bowl with lustre and cobalt blue decoration was made by Nasrid potters in Malaga, and probably commissioned by a Portuguese merchant.

'al-mulk', or 'kingship', while the vase in St Petersburg is inscribed in Arabic with the words 'pleasure', 'health' and 'benediction'.

MÁLAGA SHIP BOWL

One of the most splendid examples of early 15th-century Nasrid lustreware is a truly magnificent bowl at the Victoria and Albert Museum in London. Measuring 50cm (20in) in diameter, the lustre decoration on the interior depicts a caravel, a type of ship that was developed in the early 15th century by the Spanish and Portuguese for their voyages of exploration. The ship is shown in full sail and bearing the arms of

ancient Portugal. Perhaps the Nasrid potter was commissioned to make it by a maritime merchant from Portugal to commemorate a successful voyage. Analysis of this bowl conducted in 1983 identified the clay as Málagan and therefore of Nasrid production – before then it had been thought it came from Valencia.

After the fall of the Nasrid Empire in 1492, lustre ceramics stopped being made in Málaga. The technique was not lost though, as the lustre tradition was developed by mudéjar artists of Manises and Paterna in eastern Spain, with their famous Hispano-Moresque ceramics that flourished in the 15th and 16th centuries.

ISLAMIC ASTRONOMY AND ASTROLOGY

EVEN BEFORE THE INTRODUCTION OF ISLAM, ASTRONOMY HAD DEVELOPED THROUGHOUT THE MIDDLE EAST. CELESTIAL IMAGES, THOUGHT TO BE PROTECTIVE, WERE OFTEN USED IN DECORATION.

Above A Timurid copy of an illustration from The Book of Constellations, *by Abd al-Rahman al-Sufi, showing the constellations Centaurus and Lupus.*

Thanks to the great efforts of the translation movement in Abbasid Baghdad (8th–10th centuries), a wealth of international scientific literature had been made available for study and research in Arabic. Classical instruments, such as the celestial globe and the astrolabe, were developed further, and ancient texts in Greek, Pahlavi, Sanskrit and Syriac were drawn from and closely analysed. This intellectual culture also influenced the material world: the early 8th-century domed ceiling at the Umayyad palace of Qusayr Amra is decorated with a fresco map of the constellations.

ASTRONOMY AND ISLAM

For Muslims, astronomy held an important role in the service of Islam. The determination of daily prayer times and of the *qibla* (direction for prayer) were essential functions that scientists could address, as was calculating the lunar calendar. The appearance of a new moon, for example, signals the beginning and end of the fasting month of Ramadhan. In the 13th century, the role of the mosque astronomer (*al-muwaqqit*) was established to provide these services.

Astronomy was not restricted to only these religious purposes. Its uses in navigation and timekeeping are singled out for special praise in the Quran: 'He has ordained the night for rest and the sun and moon for reckoning. Such is the ordinance of the Mighty One, the all-knowing. It is He that has created for you the stars, so that they may guide you in the darkness of land and sea' (6:95–96). This quotation shows that practical astronomy was the norm in 7th-century Arabia, but it also emphasizes that astronomy is gifted by God – and that the stars and planets should not be venerated (as pagan deities) in themselves.

ASTRONOMY V. ASTROLOGY

In Islamic courts, there was a big demand for astronomers, who were employed not only for astronomical work (at times even teaching their patron astronomy), but also to cast horoscopes and advise the ruler of planetary events that were unusual. Because it was thought that the movements of the celestial bodies have an influence on people and objects, major events, such as laying foundations for a new palace, were planned to begin at a certain time, calculated by astronomers. For example, to guarantee a good horoscope for the Abbasids' new capital of Baghdad, two scientists were consulted before building began on 31 July 762, following their precise instructions.

Left Suleyman 'the Magnificent' founded this Istanbul observatory in 1557, and appointed the renowned scientist Taqi al-Din al-Misri as director.

Above Dedicated to Sultan Murad III, this 1583 map of the universe shows the signs of the zodiac, from Zubdet ut-Tevarih *(The Fine Flower of Histories).*

This association of astronomy (the study of celestial bodies) with astrology (the study of how these bodies influence us) was both useful and troublesome. On the one hand, rulers were most likely to sponsor major observatories and to hire astronomers in order to benefit from astrology. Also, the technical requirements of measuring the exact planetary positions in order to cast an accurate horoscope encouraged greater observational accuracy and the development of more precise instruments. On the other hand, astrology could also draw religious censure on to astronomical projects, and was used in retrospect to explain why some dynasties had fallen.

A PRINCELY ASTRONOMER

The Timurid Prince Ulugh Beg (d.1449) was more than a patron of astronomical activity: he was also a scholar, mathematician and astronomer. He built an observatory at Samarkandwhere he worked with a staff of scientists and produced new records from their observations. Ulugh Beg has been credited with designing new astronomical instruments, and a contemporary colleague described him as a proficient scientist: 'the Emperor of Islam is (himself) a learned man and the meaning of this is not said and written by way of polite custom...I venture to state that in this art he has complete mastery, and he produces elegant astronomical proofs and operations'.

Right Ulugh Beg's mural sextant at his observatory at Samarkand was used to measure the angle of celestial bodies.

CELESTIAL IMAGERY

The importance of the stars and planets in astrology guaranteed that their imagery circulated far beyond the instruments and texts of specialists in the field. The evidence found on many centuries of decorative objects, furnishings and architectural detail confirms that certain celestial bodies were widely known and respected. These are the zodiac signs, and the seven 'planets' – sun, moon, Mercury, Venus, Mars, Jupiter and Saturn – along with a 'pseudo-planet' associated with eclipses. Furthermore, astrological imagery was typically applied in an organized way, which shows that the manufacturers and indeed consumers of these luxury objects understood a set of core rules about an astrological system, which they deliberately used for their benefit.

According to astrology, each planet has zodiac constellations, where its influence will be at its most powerful. For example, the planet Mars is strongest when combined with the constellation Scorpio, and the sun when with Leo. These powerful pairings are used as decorative motifs on many luxury items of inlaid metal or overglaze-painted ceramics, as they provide the best protection and good luck to the owner.

SELJUK STONEWORK

ONE OF THE MOST OUTSTANDING FEATURES OF SELJUK BUILDINGS IS THE CARVED STONE DECORATION, ESPECIALLY ON THE PORTALS, OR ENTRANCES, WHERE MASONS CREATED AMAZINGLY DETAILED WORK.

The Anatolian Seljuks earned a reputation as great builders. Their architecture has much in common with that of their Iranian counterparts, but they created a distinctive style of their own. In part, this was due to their location. They drew some of their ideas from neighbouring Byzantium and Armenia, and they enjoyed a better supply of building material, much of it salvaged from the buildings of their vanquished enemies.

The Seljuks produced their finest work in stone. They had several grades of mason, ranging from semi-skilled artisans, who prepared roughly shaped blocks from the quarries, to gifted carvers, who produced exquisitely detailed decoration. At their best, these men produced work of outstanding quality. They mimicked the delicate stucco designs of the Great Seljuks, achieving the same lightness and grace in a harder material.

Above The calligraphy on the portal of the Ince Minareli *madrasa is intricately designed along two vertical friezes.*

CONTRASTING SURFACES

Anatolian craftsmen were fond of the contrast between large expanses of plain, smooth ashlar (square-cut stone used for facing a building) and smaller areas of compressed ornamentation. The latter was often focused around the portals of a building. This architectural approach can be found on every major structure, from mosques and *madrasas* (religious colleges) to *caravanserais* (travellers' lodges) and tombs. In many cases, the carved decoration is made in the form of a triangular, recessed arch, which has been likened to the shape of early Islamic tents.

One of the most spectacular examples can be found at the remains of the *caravanserai* between Konya and Aksaray. There, the

Left Seljuk stonemasons emphasized windows, doors and arches by framing them in receding bands of decoration. This example is from the Gök *madrasa* in Sivas, Turkey (1271).

portal contains *muqarnas* (stalactites) vaulting above carved calligraphy. Surrounding the recess, there is a shallow, rounded arch composed of interlocking geometric motifs. This, in turn, is flanked by several vertical panels of tightly packed, carved decoration. There is evidence of similar portals at the Gök *madrasa* at Sivas (1271) and the Cifte Minareli *madrasa* at Erzerum (1253).

CALLIGRAPHY IN STONE

The decoration on the Ince Minareli *madrasa* at Konya (1258) – now a museum dedicated to Seljuk stonework – is more elaborate. The entrance is framed by two bands of intertwining calligraphy and imposing sculptures.

The Ince Minareli features a mix of *naskhi* and *kufic* calligraphy, but during the Seljuk period, plaited (braided) *kufic* was the most common form. In this style of calligraphy, the lettering was interlaced in a rhythmic, ornamental fashion. The trend for plaited *kufic* script began farther east and spread west to Anatolia before the 13th century. Examples can be found on the Ince Minareli and Karatay *madrasas* in Konya, and the minaret of the Ulu Çami at Malatya.

SYMBOLIC WORK

Some of the stonework decoration may carry spiritual symbolism. A number of Seljuk buildings were adorned with panels of flowering or fruit-laden trees. In most cases, the foliage is in the form of palm leaves and the fruit, pomegranates. An eagle is often portrayed on top of the tree.

Traditionally, these emblems were interpreted as invocations of blessings, with the main image representing the Tree of Life and the bird seen as a human soul, ascending to paradise. Variants of

Above A stylized palm tree, with leaves sprouting from a crescent, adorns a panel on the Doner Kumbet, near Kayseri.

this emblem can be found on the Ince Minareli *madrasa*, the Cifte Minare *madrasa* at Erzerum and the Doner Kumbet near Kayseri.

THE TÜRBE

One fine example of a distinctive form of Seljuk architecture is the Doner Kumbet. It is a *türbe* (tomb tower), a mausoleum with a burial vault at the base and a prayer chamber above it. The shape is usually cylindrical, with a conical roof, but square or polygonal versions can be found. The exterior walls are often decorated with blind arcading (rows of arches attached to the walls), with further decoration around the base of the roof. The example at Kayseri features carvings of lions, eagles and human heads.

There is debate about the inspiration for the *türbe*. According to one long-held theory, the design of the conical roof was based on the tents used by early nomads. Other authorities see a closer parallel with the domed churches of Armenia.

SELJUK SCULPTURE

Islamic sculpture is rare, but potters in the 12th–13th century produced fine, glazed ceramic figures of animals, birds and people. The masons also created beautiful carved, high-relief stone sculpture: fine examples can be found in the northern portal of the Ince Minareli *madrasa* (1258) in Konya, where medallions and large leaves, ribbons and calligraphy bands were combined effectively. Also from Konya are pieces of high-relief figurative carving of the highest quality that once decorated the citadel built in *c*.1220 by Sultan Ala al-Din Kaykubad I. These include a two-headed eagle, elephants and crowned and winged spirits or angels.

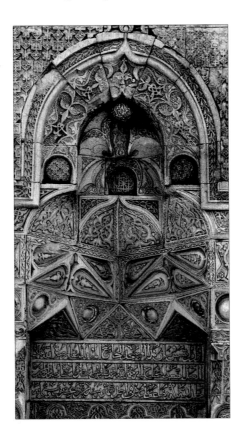

Above Calligraphy, arabesques and geometric shapes decorate the Great Mosque and Hospital at Divrigi (1229).

THE CLASSICAL ERA

CLAD WITH IZNIK TILES AND DRESSED STONE, AND EMBELLISHED WITH STAINED GLASS AND FURNITURE, 16TH-CENTURY OTTOMAN MOSQUES ARE AMONG THE GLORIES OF ISLAMIC ARCHITECTURE.

The grandeur of the classical Ottoman mosques is not only due to their vast size, ground plan and height but also to their interior decoration. The balance between light and dark, straight and curved lines, empty space and decorative excess reaches its pinnacle in the works of the master builder Sinan.

INTERIOR DECORATION
The striking colours of the tiles that adorn the buildings, commissioned from workshops in Istanbul and the town of Iznik not far from the capital, have preserved the splendour of decorative schemes from the 16th century. This is often not true of other decorative materials: few stained-glass windows have survived and the wall paintings have often been renewed several times since first executed. Contrary to current practice, it is possible that the polished marble floors were

uncovered in hot summer months, to reflect light streaming in from the windows. However, cold Istanbul winters called for warmer coverings, and the few period carpets still extant testify to the opulent, colourful woven fields of flowers and elaborate geometry added to the mosque interiors.

Sinan's Rüstem Pasha Mosque (1561–63) in Istanbul – commissioned by the Grand Wazir and son-in-law of Suleyman 'the Magnificent' – is an architecturally unassuming edifice with an ornate interior featuring a profusion of tiles arranged in panels on the walls both inside and under the front porch. The splendour and expense of the decorations enhanced the visual impact of the building.

Even more impressive is the tile cladding of the Sokollu Mehmet Pasha Mosque (1571–72), again by Sinan, for the successor of Rustem

Above The floral pattern on the tiles in the Rustem Pasha Mosque includes an innovative red colour.

Pasha. In this simple domed space with four semidomes over the side bays, the stone surfaces of the walls and bearing elements are only selectively embellished with tiles, custom-made to fit specific spaces. The beautiful effect achieved, despite the unremarkable architecture, must have been worthy compensation for the time and effort needed. The survival in more-or-less original form of the stained-glass windows completes the image of a restrained yet elegant interior.

BUILDING DONORS
The relation between the donors who funded the building of these mosques and the sultan emphasizes the social and political dimension of such religious foundations. The ruler's family and high officials erected extravagant public structures as status symbols advertising their donors' munificence and power to the capital's citizens. Women of the imperial family were also great builders. Mihrimah Sultana,

Left Calligraphy and floral patterns are among the design elements in the blue, green, red and white tiles that adorn the Sokollu Mehmet Pasha Mosque.

daughter of Suleyman 'the Magnificent' and wife of Rüstem Pasha, erected a mosque near the Edirne Gate of Istanbul's walls between 1562 and 1565. The choice of architect was unsurprising: Sinan's dense fenestration of the elevated cube under the dome dematerializes the Mihrimah Sultana Mosque's structure; he would fully deploy this decorative device a decade later in Edirne's Selimiye Mosque. The comparatively modest scale of non-sultanic buildings was a testing ground for ideas that were blended into an elegantly varied yet homogeneous body of work.

THE ARCHITECT SINAN

Sinan was the most important *mimar* (architect) in Istanbul and his long career spanning the reigns of three sultans, from the early 16th century to his death in 1588, marks the classical period of Ottoman architecture. A cross between a civil engineer, an architect and a minister of public works with a portfolio of hundreds of monuments across the Ottoman dominion, Sinan was revered even in his own lifetime.

His masterpiece is the light-filled, delicately detailed Selimiye Mosque, built in Edirne (1569–75) for Selim II (reigned 1566–74). With this mosque he claimed to have surpassed Hagia Sophia in building a larger dome. However, his real achievement is the distribution of interior space under the vast dome, which rests on eight arches supported alternately by semidomes and window-pierced walls. The arches spring from capital-free pillars that recede toward the outside of the building, creating a huge unified space unobstructed by structural elements. The multitude of glazed windows admits abundant daylight, forming an open-air, ethereal illusion. In the Selimiye Mosque, Ottoman architecture had truly surpassed its prototype, pushing the capacity of building materials and geometry to their limits.

The architecture of the late 16th and 17th centuries added few variations to the themes already introduced by Sinan and his predecessors, and there was a decline in the standards of both construction and decoration.

Above The Mihrimah Sultana Mosque in Üsküdar is another major endowment by a female member of Suleyman's family.

Above The impressive dome of the Selimiye Mosque stands 42m (138ft) tall. The slender towering minarets reach a tapered point at about 71m (233ft).

Left Pillars arranged in an octagon shape support the massive dome of the Selimiye Mosque, creating a huge area illuminated by natural daylight.

MUDÉJAR STYLE

THE DISTINCTIVE ARTISTIC STYLE OF THE MUDÉJARS FLOURISHED
IN THE ARCHITECTURE AND DECORATIVE ARTS OF SPAIN FROM
THE 14TH TO THE 16TH CENTURIES.

Those Muslims who stayed in Spain after the end of Islamic rule and the Christian 'Reconquista' in 1492 were known as the mudéjars. The word 'mudéjar' is probably a medieval Spanish corruption of the Arabic word *al-mudajjanun*, meaning 'those permitted to remain'. During this period, the new Christian rulers were under pressure to repopulate the lands they had conquered, to irrigate and farm the lands and to create vital tax revenue. The mudéjars were allowed to continue practising their religion, customs and language under Christian rule.

The Christian aristocracy, who wanted to emulate the sophisticated art and architecture of the previous Muslim rulers, became patrons of the mudéjar artisans. Even the Catholic monarchs of the Reconquista, Ferdinand and Isabella, commissioned works of mudéjar

craftsmanship, including lustreware and carpets. The craftsmen, who sometimes formed guilds, worked in masonry, carpentry, textiles, ceramics and metalwork, areas in which they had amazing technical proficiency. Mudéjar style is characterized by its integration of Islamic decorative style with elements from the Christian arts.

ARCHITECTURE

The new Christian kings and noblemen were fascinated with the luxury and refinement associated with the Islamic style. New palaces were built and old ones renovated by mudéjar craftsmen, who created royal residences in brick, wood and plaster. The 11th-century Islamic fortified palace of Aljaferia in Saragossa was substantially renovated in the 14th century by mudéjar artists working for King Pedro IV. The Alcazar of Seville was

Above These tiles from the Santa Cruz district of Seville are in the mudéjar *style. Tin-glazed and decorated ceramic tiles like these are known as* azulejos.

rebuilt in 1364 for the Christian ruler Pedro I, emulating the style of the Islamic palaces of al-Andalus, with patios and ornamented façades, carved wooden doors, fountains, elaborately carved stucco and even Arabic inscriptions referring to Pedro I as 'sultan'.

The mudéjars were responsible for religious as well as aristocratic and secular art, as Islamic motifs invoked notions of power and wealth in the church as well as the palace to a population that had until recently lived under Islamic rule. In synagogues and cathedrals, they used brick and wood instead of stone as a primary material. The magnificent painted wooden ceiling of Teruel Cathedral in Aragon is a masterpiece of the mudéjar style from the late 13th century. A look up to the ceiling

Left In 1364, the Alcazar of Seville was rebuilt in Islamic style for the Christian ruler, Pedro I.

above the nave reveals a lively and colourful mix of scenes from everyday life, with musicians, knights on horseback, animals and even a group of carpenters.

Mudéjar craftsmen also worked for Jewish patrons, in buildings such as the 'el Transito' synagogue in Toledo. This prayer hall was built in the mid-14th century by mudéjars working for Samuel Halevi Abulafia, tax collector for King Pedro I. Beautifully detailed inscriptions in Arabic and Hebrew are finely carved in stucco on the walls.

CERAMICS

Mudéjar ceramics reached a high point both aesthetically and commercially in the lustreware made in the villages of Manises and Paterna just outside Valencia. Their distinctive ceramics, known as 'Hispano-Moresque' ware, combined motifs from Islamic culture, such as pseudo-Arabic inscriptions and arabesques, with Christian elements

Above This elaborate mudéjar ceiling, built after 1504, is in the monastery of San Juan de los Reyes, in Toledo.

of heraldry and cartouches with Christian inscriptions, to create a distinctive mudéjar aesthetic.

The early pieces were greatly influenced by Nasrid ceramics. It is thought that potters from Nasrid Granada may have emigrated to Manises in the early 14th century at the request of Pedro Buyl, Lord of Manises. Demand outstripped supply as potters began to work on a level approaching mass production. They worked for a wealthy Christian clientele and made plates, bowls, basins, pharmacy jars and pots meant for everyday use. Italian nobility soon became the largest market for Manises lustreware. In fact, many surviving

Right A Hispano-Moresque dish with lustre and cobalt blue decoration, made in Manises in the 15th century.

objects are datable by the Italian coats of arms that decorate them. Images of Manises ceramics are even found in Renaissance paintings from as early as the 15th century.

Mudéjar art declined in Spain during the 16th century, and finally disappeared at the time of the forced conversions, and finally expulsions of Muslims in 1609–10.

CARVINGS, METALWORK, COSTUME AND CARPETS

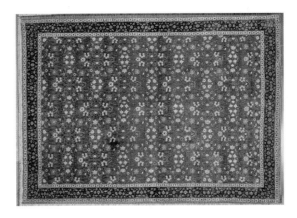

This chapter describes how skilled artisans throughout the centuries carved superb pieces from materials such as rock crystal, wood, ivory and jade, how they produced metalwork decorated with gold and silver inlay, and how they created ceremonial silk costumes and luxurious woven carpets.

Opposite *This early 18th-century Mughal miniature painting depicts a noblewoman wearing earrings and a necklace made with pearls, emeralds and red spinels.*

Above *This carpet features a floral design organized in a tight lattice.*

UMAYYAD COINS

AFTER INITIALLY MAKING ONLY MINOR AMENDMENTS TO THE COINAGE OF THEIR PREDECESSORS, THE UMAYYAD CALIPHS GRADUALLY DEVELOPED NEW DESIGNS THAT WERE DISTINCTIVELY ISLAMIC.

Coins known as the dinar and dirham are mentioned in the Quran, but scholars believe that the Arabs had very little of their own money in circulation in Arabia. However, when they took over the government of the former Sasanian and Byzantine empires, the Umayyads understood the importance of continuity in economic matters. To maintain healthy levels of trade, it was essential that merchants had confidence in the coinage, and a sudden change to unfamiliar designs might have endangered this.

ECONOMIC CONTINUITY

The earliest surviving Arab coins in fact just predate the Umayyad era (661–750). These early coins are marked 653, which is 21 years after the Prophet's death in 632 and 8 years before the establishment of the Umayyad Caliphate by Muawiyah I in 661.

When they first came to power, the Umayyads kept familiar coins in circulation. Umayyad coins minted in former Sasanian territory (Iran and Iraq) were adaptations of Sasanian silver coinage; they continued to feature the head of the Sasanian Shah Khosrow II (reigned 590–628) on the front and – because the Sasanian kings followed the Zoroastrian religion – a Zoroastrian fire altar appeared on the reverse.

The Umayyads seem to have continued using Iranian die-makers to mint their coins. The coins bore the mint marks and sometimes the name of the Arab governor in the *pahlavi* script that had been used by the Sasanians.

The date of issue was given both in the Sasanian reckoning and in the Hijra calendar (counted from the Prophet Muhammad's migration from Makkah to Madinah in 622). However, Umayyad rulers also clearly felt the need to promote the Islamic faith that was driving their imperial expansion and coins began to appear incorporating pious Muslim doctrinal slogans in *kufic* script, such as 'All praise be to Allah' and 'In Allah's name'.

Left A coin from the reign of the second Sasanian king, Shapur I (reigned 241–72), features the Zoroastrian fire altar.

***Above** This silver drachm bears the head of Sasanian monarch Khosrow II. The Arab conquerors of Iran kept coins of this type in circulation.*

BYZANTINE INHERITANCE

In Syria, which had previously been part of the Byzantine Empire, the Arab conquerors also initially issued coins identical in appearance to those of their forerunner. The coins bore images of Byzantine imperial figures, including Emperor Heraclius (reigned 610–41) with his sons. As in Iraq and Iran, the Umayyad rulers had decided to keep the coins looking as similar as possible in the interests of continuity, but they gradually began to make minor changes in order to nullify the Christian symbols used on the coins. For example, they removed the horizontal arm of the crucifix found on the back of some coins, or they cut out the 'I' from the monogram 'ICXC' used to represent Christ's name in orthodox Christianity.

In time, the figure of the Byzantine ruler was replaced with a turbaned and clearly Arab male, standing and holding a sword. This figure has been interpreted by some scholars as an image of the caliph giving the *khutbah* sermon at Friday prayers, and the coins have become known as 'standing caliph' coins.

On the reverse they bore an image of the lance associated with the Prophet, set within a niche – clearly a modification of the Christian image of the cross standing at the top of a flight of steps that appeared on Byzantine coins. According to Islamic tradition, the lance was given to one of the Prophet's companions by an Ethiopian ruler and it was then passed on to Muhammad himself; the image was used in the first mosques to indicate the direction of Makkah. The niche on the coin, although it may appear to suggest the *mihrab* prayer niche found in mosques, is most likely a reference to niches in Byzantine architecture as *mihrabs* were probably not yet in use in mosques.

AN ISLAMIC COINAGE

In around 696–98, Islamic coinage was reformed under Umayyad Caliph Abd al-Malik, builder of the Dome of the Rock in Jerusalem. A new weight standard was set for coins, and all figurative images were replaced with Islamic messages written in Arabic *kufic* script. The

AFTER THE UMAYYADS

The style of coins introduced in the late 7th century under the Umayyad caliphs was the standard one used to produce Muslim coinage for several hundred years, and was used also by the Umayyads' Abbasid successors. The name of the ruling caliph was generally not included on the coins until the Abbasid era, beginning with those issued by al-Mahdi (reigned 775–85). Thereafter, it became standard practice to include the name of the reigning caliph on coins.

purpose of the epigraphs was to remind all subjects of the empire of the success and supremacy of the conquerors' Islamic faith.

Just as the interior of the Dome of the Rock was emblazoned with mosaic messages that set Islamic beliefs apart from Christian and Jewish doctrines, so the new gold dinars issued by Abd al-Malik declared the key beliefs that differentiated Islam from rival faiths. The coins bore doctrinal statements, such as the *kalimah* ('words') *La ilahu illa Allah, wa Muhammad rasul Allah* ('There is no god but Allah, and Muhammad is Allah's Messenger'), and directly dismissed the concept that Christ is

(in the words of the biblical Gospel of John) 'the only begotten Son of God', declaring 'Allah has no associate' and 'Allah does not beget, and was never begotten'. There were two denominations of coins: the copper fals and the silver dirham. Although there was a great variety in the issues of the lesser copper coins, there was remarkable uniformity among the silver dirhams, all of which bore calligraphy of the same type. All the coins bore a date and the name of the mint at which they were struck.

Below These 10th-century coins show that epigraphy became the dominant theme of Islamic coinage.

ROCK CRYSTAL

THE FATIMIDS VALUED ROCK CRYSTAL BOTH FOR ITS BEAUTY AND ITS 'MAGICAL' POWERS. ASTOUNDING QUANTITIES OF THIS PRIZED MATERIAL WERE FOUND IN THE FATIMID TREASURY.

Several deposits of rock crystal, a transparent quartz, can be found across the Middle East and Asia. Writing in the early 11th century, the Persian scholar and scientist al-Biruni stated that the finest pieces of rock crystal were produced at Basra in Iraq and that the raw material was imported from the Laccadive and Maldive islands and from the islands of Zanj in East Africa. The Iranian traveller Nasir-i Khusrau, who visited Cairo in 1046 and saw rock crystal being carved in the lamp market, mentions that Yemen was the source of the purest rock crystal but that lesser quality crystal was also imported from North Africa and India.

THE CRAFTSMEN

Rock crystal is a hard mineral that requires great expertise to carve. Skilled lapidaries from Basra probably migrated to Cairo to seek the patronage of the Fatimid court, just as the potters are known to have done. The craftsmen cut blocks of crystal roughly the shape of the vessel they intended to make and then laboriously drilled out the interior, leaving walls of remarkable thinness before carving the decoration and polishing the exterior.

Right Carvings of a large bird of prey attacking a horned deer appear on this 10th–11th-century ewer from Cairo. The carvings symbolize the power of the ruler over his enemies.

THE FATIMID TREASURY

When the Fatimid palace was looted in 1068–69, many of the valuable artefacts that had been concealed in the storerooms were dispersed. The *Kitab al-Hadaya wa al-Tuhaf* (Book of Gifts and Rarities), compiled in the 11th century, refers to the gifts exchanged between Muslim and non-Muslim rulers and officials. It contains an eyewitness account of some of the items that were removed. The author refers to 36,000 objects of glass and rock crystal that were found in the treasury, but also lists a number

Above A crescent carved from rock crystal is mounted in a 14th-century European silver and enamel monstrance. A kufic inscription carved into the crystal gives the name of the Fatimid Caliph al-Zahir.

of specific rock-crystal objects, including a spouted ewer of smooth rock crystal with a handle carved from the same block, a large storage jar with images carved in high relief, and a box with a lid cut from a single block of rock crystal, made to store small rock crystal dishes.

The same source that listed the precious items dispersed from the Fatimid treasury also described how these objects were sold in the local markets and bazaars and also sold to the courts of neighbouring countries, such as Spain and Sicily, as well as the Byzantine court in Constantinople. Many of these rock-crystal pieces ended up in church treasuries across Europe, often as containers for storing saintly relics.

SURVIVING TREASURES

Several of the surviving pieces contain inscriptions naming their patrons, who include two caliphs and a general. Eight complete ewers have survived, each one of similar pear-shaped form, carved with pairs of animals beside scrolling foliage and with an intricately pierced handle topped with an animal as a thumb rest. One of these ewers, now in the treasury of San Marco in Venice, Italy, bears a dedicatory inscription to Caliph al-Aziz (reigned 975–96). It is carved with face-to-face lions, the quintessential symbol of royalty. Another ewer, decorated with a pair of birds with elegant curving necks and long beaks, was commissioned for Husayn ibn Jawhar, a general of Caliph al-Hakim. The final inscribed piece is a curious crescent-shaped object that may have been mounted on a horse's bridle as a royal emblem; it contains the titles of Caliph al-Zahir (reigned 1021–36). Other types of objects made from rock crystal include lamps, small bottles that probably contained precious oils, chess pieces and small animal figures.

Right This rock crystal ewer from Fatimid Cairo, carved with a pair of birds below a kufic *inscription, is now in the Musée du Louvre, Paris.*

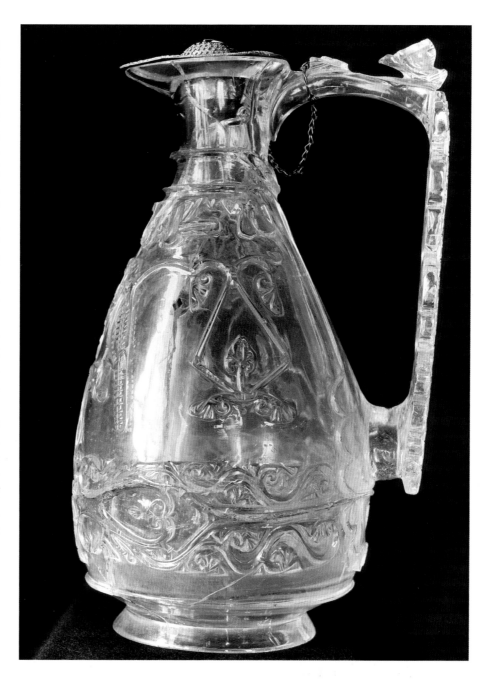

MAGICAL LINKS

Although rock crystal was valued for its aesthetic qualities, it was also held in great esteem by the Fatimids, along with other cultures, because they believed it had magical properties linked with its similarity to water and air. In fact, the Arabic name for 'rock crystal', *maha*, is a synthesis of the two components of which it was believed to be made: *ma,* or 'water' and *hawa,* or 'air'. The Persian-born author and judge al-Qazwini (1203–83) explained that kings preferred to drink out of rock-crystal vessels because they had the power to prevent them from ever becoming thirsty. In the Quran, there are two passages that describe how cups of rock crystal filled with pure water will be offered to the believers in paradise.

Left This rock crystal ewer, now broken, was inscribed with the titles of Husayn ibn Jawhar, a general of Caliph al-Hakim who held the title from 1000 until 1008.

WOOD AND IVORY CARVING

THE SKILLED ARTISANS OF FATIMID EGYPT CREATED SUPERB CARVED WOOD AND IVORY PIECES, PRODUCING INTRICATE ABSTRACT GEOMETRIC DESIGNS AND LIVELY FIGURAL DEPICTIONS.

Several beautiful carved wooden friezes once graced the lavish Western Palace of the Fatimid caliphs in Cairo. The palace was abandoned after the fall of the Fatimid dynasty in 1171, and later made part of the Hospital of the Mamluk Sultan Qalawun (completed 1284). The friezes were discovered by chance during restoration work on the hospital, and, remarkably, are all that survives of the once magnificent setting of the Fatimid court as described in medieval accounts.

SECULAR WOODCARVING

The surviving fragments are typical of Fatimid secular woodcarving in representing the pleasures of court life, such as hunting, musical entertainment, dancing and drinking wine. Human and animal figures are framed by winding plant tendrils or interlaced geometric patterns, and sometimes also by bands of calligraphic inscriptions.

One splendid frieze depicts a hunter spearing a lion and a courtier pouring wine while another plays a pipe. It has a recurring image of long-eared hares and a perched bird, a characteristic element in Fatimid figurative decorations. Fragments of paint found on the frieze suggest that it was once coloured blue with the figures highlighted in red.

Another frieze shows two gazelles, with beautifully fluid heads, horns and haunches. The figurative representations of animals and people

Above *Fluid horses' necks and heads emerge from a delicate geometric pattern on this teak door panel carved by Fatimid artisans in the 11th century.*

produced by Fatimid artists in wood-carving are generally more fluid and vital than the stiff images created by earlier Islamic craftsmen.

CARVED *MIHRABS*

One of the best surviving examples of sacred woodcarving is the *mihrab* from the Mausoleum of Sayyida Ruqayya in the Southern Cemetery in Cairo, built in 1154–60. Sayyida Ruqayya was a daughter of Ali, husband of the Prophet's daughter Fatima, though another of Ali's wives was her mother. She went to Cairo with her stepsister Zaynab and the two women are seen as being among the city's patron saints.

Sayyida Ruqayya's tomb is a *mashhad*, or pilgrimage shrine, much visited by Shiah Muslims. The *mihrab* has been removed from the shrine and is housed in the Islamic Museum in Cairo, but a fine wooden screen remains in the shrine.

Another beautiful wooden *mihrab* now in the museum was taken from the Fatimid shrine to Sayyida Nafisa (great-granddaughter of the Prophet's grandson Hasan), who died

Left *This portable* mihrab *(1133) from the Mausoleum of Sayyida Ruqayya has wooden panels carved with six-pointed stars, a design known as the star-shaped medallion.*

in Fustat in 824. While alive, she gained a reputation for piety and for performing miracles, and during the Fatimid era her shrine was a great attraction for Shiah pilgrims, who sought to benefit from her *baraka* (divine blessing).

Fatimid wooden panels and fragments of friezes carved with animals also survive. Two rectangular panels, probably originally set within a door, are deeply carved with the sinuous necks and heads of a pair of horses, each wearing a decorated bridle. The panels were carved to different depths, a skilled technique mastered by Fatimid craftsmen and used to work both wood and ivory. One panel is in the Metropolitan Museum, New York, and the other in the Islamic Museum in Cairo.

LUXURY WORK

Whereas in some parts of the Islamic world, such as Turkey and northern Iran, wood was common and was used as a basic building material, in Egypt it was scarce; the woods used for the fine Fatimid carvings that have survived, which include acacia, box, cedar, cypress, ebony, pine and teak, would all have been imported.

As well as palace friezes and internal mosque features, such as wall-mounted wooden *mihrabs*, the woodcarvers of the Fatimid court also produced ceiling rafters, door panels, mosque furniture, caskets and portable *mihrabs*. Large pieces were inlaid with ivory. Wooden furniture and fittings from mosques were often reused not only because the wood was scarce but also because it had acquired a degree of sanctity from its sacred setting.

IVORY CARVINGS

Fatimid Egypt was a great centre for ivory carving in the Islamic world because of its proximity to the main source of the material in East Africa. Craftsmen in Egypt were concentrated in Fustat in particular, but Fatimid ivory carvers were also at work in what are now Tunisia and Sicily.

Carvers produced inlay panels to decorate objects made from wood, together with small ivory items, such as caskets, combs and chess pieces. They also carved delicate decorations on to pieces of elephant tusk. Initially, only the broad end of the tusk was decorated, but later examples are carved along the whole length. These items – which are often called 'oliphants' from the archaic English word for 'elephant' – were exported to many countries of Christian Europe.

Larger ivory carvings – intended to be inset in wooden furniture or used as room decoration – were similar in style to

Left This carved ivory figure was made at Fustat, Egypt, the principal centre of ivory carving in Fatimid times.

Above This detail from a Fatimid ivory plaque in the Museum of Islamic Art in Berlin shows a figure drinking at a banquet.

those found on woodcarving. They represented scenes of court life featuring huntsmen and animals, dancers and musicians, all so delicately rendered that the details of an animal's fur or the fall of a dancer's costume can be clearly seen.

Four ivory panels in Berlin are carved with a range of different figures enjoying the pleasures of a banquet with wine and musical entertainment all set against a sinuous vine scroll dripping with bunches of grapes. Whether working in wood or ivory, the Fatimid artisans demonstrated a supreme mastery of their materials.

SPANISH IVORIES

THE INTRICATELY CARVED IVORIES OF ISLAMIC SPAIN ARE EVIDENCE OF THE ARTISTIC AND TECHNICAL EXPERTISE REACHED BY CRAFTSMEN DURING THE 10TH AND 11TH CENTURIES.

Craftsmen turned pieces of elephant ivory into small containers, and carved them with beautiful calligraphic inscriptions and lively depictions of birds, animals, gardens and human figures. The earliest Spanish carved ivories were made at Madinat al-Zahra, the Umayyad royal city near Córdoba, in the mid-10th century, at the height of the Caliphate. Ivory was carved into two shapes: either into a casket, a small box with a flat or pitched lid, or into a cylindrical container with a domed lid known as a pyxis.

ROYAL COMMISSIONS

The tradition of ivory carving spread from ancient Syria and Egypt to Spain in the Islamic period. The royal court at Madinat al-Zahra commanded vast wealth and monopolized the ivory industry of Islamic Spain. They imported tusks of ivory from its source in East Africa and received ivory as gifts from foreign royalty. It was reported that 3,630kg (8,000lb) of the most pure ivory was sent as part of a present to Caliph al-Hisham II by a Berber prince in 991.

The craftsmen worked in royal workshops with the finest ivory to create their unique objects, often working in teams. The pyxides were carved on a lathe, while the caskets were constructed from 1-cm (½-in) thick plaques sawn from the tusk and fitted to a wooden frame. They were carved in relief with sharp chisel-like tools.

INSCRIPTIONS

An Arabic inscription was often carved around the lid of the completed ivories in foliate script.

These often tell us the place, for whom and when they were made and sometimes even the name of the craftsmen. Most of the ivories were specially commissioned for members of the caliph's family or courtly entourage. However, one pyxis at London's Victoria and Albert Museum was made for the prefect of police, while two pyxides and two flat boxes were made in 964 and 966 for a lady called Subh. She was a Basque from Gascony, the consort of Caliph al-Hakam II and mother of his son and successor al-Hisham II. The poetic inscription on another pyxis in the Hispanic Society of America hints that these luxury objects were used as containers to store precious jewels, spices and unguents:

Above *A detail of an ivory casket, with peacock designs, made for the concubine of Caliph al-Hakam II, Subh.*

Above *This intricately carved lid from 999 bears the name of Sanchuelo, second son of Caliph al-Mansur.*

'Beauty has invested me with
splendid raiment,
Which makes a display of jewels.
I am a receptacle for musk,
camphor and ambergris.'

AL-MUGHIRA PYXIS

The 'al-Mughira' pyxis was made in 968 and is a masterpiece of intricate design and skill. It was made for Prince al-Mughira, second son of Abd al-Rahman III and considered a hopeful for the throne of his brother al-Hakam.

The carvings on the pyxis are not fully understood. They might show scenes from the life of the prince, or perhaps they celebrate seasonal festivals or pursuits. Four cartouches, read from right to left, start under the beginning of the inscription, with the image of a youth reaching up to steal eggs from three eagles' nests. The second image shows a lute player flanked by two barefoot youths, while the third and fourth scenes show lions attacking bulls and a pair of youths on horseback picking dates from a tree. These images are surrounded by smaller vignettes of wrestlers, wolves, fighting animals and pairs of birds, filled in with delicately intertwining leaves, resulting in an intricate mix of agricultural and hunting images.

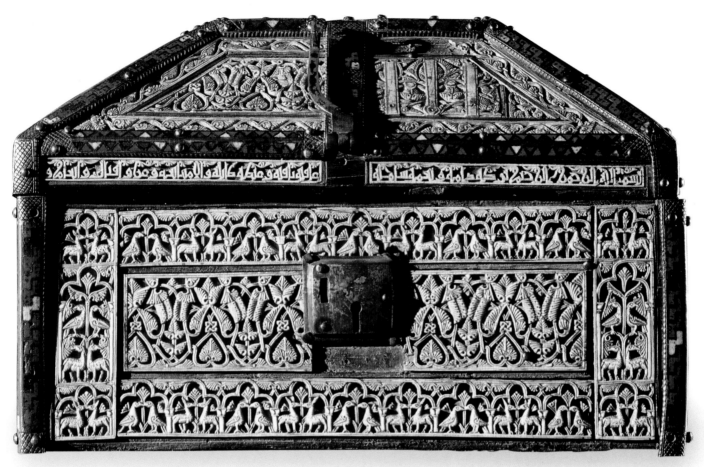

Above This ivory casket was made in 1049–50 in the Cuenca workshops, and signed by a member of the Ibn Zayyan family. The enamel mounts are later European additions.

PAMPLONA CASKET

With the decline of the caliph's power in the late 10th century, production of luxury carved ivory moved to Córdoba, where the ambitious chamberlain al-Mansur commissioned a superb casket, which is now in Pamplona.

Al-Mansur had virtually taken over the rule of al-Andalus from the weakened caliph, and the depiction of the chamberlain in royal guise seated on a throne and flanked by attendants is an obvious display of this new authority. The signatures of a whole team of craftsmen are

Right The Pamplona casket, dated 1004, has elaborately carved panels showing the seated ruler and figures playing musical instruments.

hidden throughout this casket. One of them, Misbah, even carved his name on the throne platform under the chamberlain's feet.

THE CUENCA IVORIES

In the 11th century, when al-Andalus was fragmented into *taifas* (small kingdoms), the carved ivory workshops moved from Córdoba to Cuenca, where craftsmen worked under the ruling family known as the Dhu'l-Nunids. The ivories the family commissioned were made by single craftsmen, such as Ibn Zayyan, who signed the 'Silos' casket of 1026–27. The Cuenca ivories are less richly carved than the earlier ivories, with simple repetitive decorations.

JADE CARVING

IN THE ISLAMIC PERIOD, JADE CARVING WAS WIDESPREAD IN TIMURID IRAN AND IN MUGHAL INDIA. THE RAW MATERIAL WAS ACQUIRED FROM KHOTAN IN CENTRAL ASIA.

Jade has always been noted for its medicinal qualities, a tradition that in China dates back into prehistory. Medieval Arabic and Persian texts describe a wide range of apotropaic and medicinal properties, ranging from victory in battle, protection from lightning and earthquakes, the prevention and cure of illness, and repelling the effects of poison.

WORKING WITH JADE

The jade of objects crafted in Iran and India was nephrite. It is found in a wide range of colours; most commonly in shades of green, but also brown, yellow and red, and a translucent white, the rarest and most sought-after type of all.

To create a vessel, the raw jade is sawed into blocks of a workable size and shaped into the desired form using a hand-operated lathe. Then, the surface is polished using various stone, leather and wooden surfaces, together with abrasive substances to create the desired smoothness. Lastly, the object is often, but not always, decorated with inlays of different precious metals and gemstones.

TIMURID JADE

The main source of jade was in the Kunlun mountains near Khotan in Central Asia, which, in the 15th century, was within the Timurid Empire. It is from this period (1370–1506) that the production of Islamic jades became established.

A number of jade objects are associated with Timur and his descendants. The cenotaph of Timur in the Gur-e Amir is carved from a massive single block of dark green jade brought from Mongolia by his grandson Ulugh Beg.

Two notable jade vessels are inscribed with the name of this ruler: a shallow cup kept in the British Museum, London, is made of green jade with a handle in the form of a Chinese hornless dragon,

Above A dagger handle made from nephrite jade, set with gold and rubies. It dates from the reign of the Mughal Emperor, Alamgir (reigned 1658–1707).

and a pot-bellied jug has a sinuous handle in the form of this same mythical creature.

MUGHAL JADE

The true heirs of the Timurid tradition can be found in India, at the Mughal court, where the work was often carried out by expatriate Persian artists. Jade carving flourished during the rule of Jahangir (reigned 1605–27) and his son Shah Jahan (reigned 1628–57), and continued throughout the 18th century.

The Mughal court chronicler Abu'l Fazl records that a merchant named Khwaja Muin, was received

Left This white jade Mughal wine cup is carved so thinly that it appears translucent.

Right *A 19th-century jade mirror-back set with precious stones. The floral pattern is reminiscent of designs that can be found in Islamic metalwork, textiles and tiles.*

Right *A 19th-century jade mirror-back set with precious stones. The floral pattern is reminiscent of designs that can be found in Islamic metalwork, textiles and tiles.*

at the court of Akbar (reigned 1556–1605). He controlled the jade monopoly at Kashgar and is said to have stopped at the court with a selection of his wares, while en route to Makkah to perform the pilgrimage. Some sources pinpoint the start of the trend more specifically, linking it with the visit of Khwaja Mucin, who was the grandfather of one of Akbar's (reigned 1556–1605) generals. He controlled the jade monopoly at Kashgar and is said to have stopped at the Mughal court during a pilgrimage to Makkah, with a selection of his wares.

Mughal patrons commissioned a number of jade vessels that carry echoes of the work produced in central Asia. In the British Museum in London, for example, there is a fine cup in the shape of a gourd, which was made for Shah Jahan (reigned 1628–58) in 1647. Dating from the same period, there is also a jade box formed into the shape of a mango.

Increasingly, jade was used as a component of fine jewellery and ceremonial armour. There are many great 17th- and 18th-century examples of daggers produced with elaborate jade handles encrusted with jewels.

The Mughal emperor honoured his princes and high-ranking officials with the gift of such daggers; these were

worn tucked into the waist sash, as highly visible symbols of the owner's status and wealth. Mughal artists produced an extraordinary range of lavish jade plaques. These were used to adorn a variety of objects, from bow cases to belts, and Quran bindings to mirror-backs. Typifying this trend is a sumptuous jade mirror, now housed in the Victoria and Albert Museum in London. The octagonal object, fashioned out of green jade, is decorated with flower-shaped inlays made out of white jade, and is encrusted with gold mounts and rubies.

Right *A jade dish, produced in India in the 18th century. Luxury items were in high demand at the Mughal court and the simplest household goods were often fashioned out of jade or crystal.*

KHURASAN INLAID METALWORK

IN 12TH-CENTURY KHURASAN, LUXURY COPPER-ALLOY OBJECTS WERE DECORATED FIRST WITH ENGRAVED CHASED PATTERNS, AND THEN WITH INLAID PRECIOUS METALS.

The period from the 12th to 14th centuries saw great innovations in the technique and style of inlaid metalwork. Production centres appeared first in the Khurasan province of north-east Iran, and from the 13th century in Mosul (Iraq) and elsewhere, where the technique of inlaying brass or bronze objects with silver, copper and eventually gold details was developed to a high level, rivalling the detailed surface decoration found on contemporary ceramics, glass and even manuscripts.

On an ostentatious level, the precious metal inlays added value to an object, with the base metal acquiring the glittering surface of a more precious metal. Emulation of more expensive materials also seems to have occurred in contemporary ceramics, which used lustre glazes to echo the gleam of metal and imitated metal shapes.

INLAYING METAL

Metal inlay is a technique in which a softer and more precious metal is applied to the surface of a cheaper, stronger metal or alloy. The receiving surface is usually lightly punched to make a pockmarked area, and the softer metal is then hammered on, thus easing it into the punched grooves for a more secure grip. The technique could be used to enhance a pattern or inscription engraved on to a metal object, highlighting the lines of script, clarifying a design or framed area, or bringing up the main characters in a figural scene. Dense pictorial detail, elaborate

calligraphic inscriptions, along with sophisticated floral and geometric patterns, were all applied to metal vessels, transforming the style of previous generations of metalwork.

FORM AND FUNCTION

Khurasan metalwork was made in a wide range of forms and functions, but most of these objects were made for hospitality uses in wealthy homes, such as ewers, cups and incense-burners, or for official use, such as pen boxes and caskets. Many pieces of Khurasan metalwork, such as the Bobrinsky bucket (see opposite page), were produced by casting them in a mould. Casting allows for more sculptural variety and flexibility in the final shape, and spectacular pieces, such as a cow, calf and lion group, demonstrate great

Above The c.1200 *Vaso Vescovali is a cast brass bowl made in Khurasan. The silver inlaid lid is contemporary to the bowl but from a separate object.*

technical skill. According to its own inscription, all three animals were cast simultaneously. Although it is sometimes said that Islamic art features no three-dimensional sculpture, there are many functional objects that contradict this claim, such as a feline incense-burner (see opposite page).

Right This cast brass animal group, in the form of a cow, calf, and lion, is a ewer, dated 1206. It has silver inlay and is engraved with a frieze along the flanks.

Below The body of this 11th-century cast brass incense-burner, in the shape of a lion, has a pierced openwork pattern as well as holes for the eyes and mouth, through which smoke could pass.

DECORATIVE THEMES

The theme of courtly pleasures is ubiquitous in Islamic art of the 12th to 13th centuries, but a second recurring theme, that of astrology, echoed the benevolent wishes so frequently inscribed on luxury goods. Figures symbolizing the planets were often depicted in combination with zodiac signs, showing each planet at its most powerful and useful position, thus invoking good associations for the owners of the metal object. The Vaso Vescovali cast brass bowl features astrology as its main theme, and also includes a minor frieze depicting a party with musical entertainment and drinking guests.

These metal objects usually bore a formal inscription that delivered a consistent formula of good wishes directed at an unnamed owner, such as 'Glory and Prosperity', 'Power', 'Safety', 'Happiness',

'Success' or 'Blessings'. Because inscriptions rarely mention the owner by name, it is thought that these luxury objects were produced for the open market, not for a court context.

While silver or copper could be used to brighten some parts of a design, black substances, such as niello, bitumen or mastic, were sometimes used simultaneously to darken engraved lines. This allowed the metalworker to create a more graphic range of colour contrast.

The stylistic developments that occurred throughout this period meant that engraved designs were becoming increasingly sophisticated on Islamic metalwork. In unskilled hands, these developments could have led to an eventual incoherence of the overall design; however, small areas or lines accented with metal inlay were used as a new way to clarify the design.

THE BOBRINKSY BUCKET

A key piece of Khurasan inlaid metalwork is known as the Bobrinsky bucket, made in Herat in 1163. This remarkable bucket, for use in a bathhouse, is decorated with several layers of inlaid silver and copper, depicting the lively pleasures of drinking, enjoying music, dancing and hunting on horseback. It bears many inscriptions, mainly with the standard long formula of good wishes (such as 'Glory and Prosperity'), but also with the date, names of the patron and commissioning agent, and those of the metalworker and the inlayer. The owner is described as the 'pride of the merchants, trusted by the Muslims, ornament of the pilgrimage and the two sanctuaries', and was evidently a well-travelled merchant and *Hajj* pilgrim.

Above The densely inscribed Bobrinsky bucket is a cast brass bucket with silver and copper inlay decoration and a handle.

INLAID METALWORK OF MOSUL

IN THE EARLY 13TH CENTURY, ACCOMPLISHED INLAID METALWORK BEGAN TO BE PRODUCED IN MOSUL IN NORTHERN IRAQ, POSSIBLY AS A RESULT OF SKILLED CRAFTSMEN EMIGRATING FROM IRAN.

The production of precious metal inlay, in which expensive metal is used to decorate the surface of a cheaper metal alloy object, was highly developed in the Khurasan province of eastern Iran. This production seems to have shifted to the city of Mosul, northern Iraq, around the same time that Mongol invasions led by Genghis Khan were creating an impact on cities in north-eastern Iran. Samarkand, Merv, Nishapur and Herat were devastated in the early 1220s, and their citizens massacred. A contemporary historian, Ibn al-Athir, described these dramatic events:

'In just one year [the Mongols] seized the most populous, most beautiful and the best cultivated part of the earth whose characters excelled in civilization and urbanity. In the countries which have not yet been overrun by them, everyone spends the night afraid they may appear there too.'

The sudden shift of metal inlay production has been interpreted as the result of the emigration of Khurasanis fleeing the Mongols. Certainly, the ruination of the region would mean that the local market for luxury wares was damaged, and it

Above This inlaid brass basin, made for Ayyubid Sultan al-Adil II Abu Bakr in 1238–40, is decorated with vivid scenes of hunters and animals.

would make economic sense for producers to move to richer and less turbulent areas in western Iran and Iraq. Most Mosul metalwork is dated later than the invasion of Khurasan, and some signatures show direct connections with the Khurasani producers. One 1229 ewer confirms this connection: it is signed 'Iyas assistant of Abu'l-Karim b. al-Turabi al-Mawsili'. 'Turabi' refers to the city of Merv in north-eastern Iran, and 'Mawsili' refers to the master's new home in Mosul.

AL-MAWSILI, OR 'OF MOSUL'
The metal inlay craftsmen of Mosul often signed their wares using the *nisba*, or toponym, *al-Mawsili*, meaning 'of Mosul'. However, throughout the 13th century and into the early 14th, this *nisba* features on many inlaid metal objects that were made in other places, such as Egypt and Syria. It appears that *al-Mawsili* refers to the craftsman's place of training and its specific reputation, not necessarily where the object was produced.

Mosul inlaid metal objects usually feature lively figural scenes of people or animals, either in long narrow friezes or more often in vignettes within cartouches (a type

Left Dinner guests, musicians and dancers are the main decorative subjects on this 13th-century candlestick, made from brass with silver inlay.

Above The Blacas Ewer, made in Mosul in 1232, is a masterpiece of inlaid metalwork. The vignettes show scenes of court life, hunting and war.

MOSUL DIASPORA

Only one dated Mosul object is inscribed with the statement that it was produced in Mosul itself: this is the Blacas Ewer, dated 1232, now in the British Museum. It is signed by one Shuja b. Mana al-Mawsili 'in Mosul', and the ewer may have been made for the city's ruler Badr al-Din Lulu (d.1259). It is an object of outstanding quality, decorated with a series of framed scenes, laid in horizontal bands that draw from the 'princely cycle' repertoire of hunting and feasting, as well as astrological figures, calligraphy, and decorative scrollwork and patterns.

There are just six other known objects that most likely come from Mosul itself, as they belonged to Badr al-Din Lulu or members of his court. The *nisba* signature of *al-Mawsili*, however, is on at least 28 known inlaid metal objects, as a diaspora of metalworkers trained in Mosul was active in the rest of Jazira province and further south in the courts of Ayyubid Syria and Egypt. It reflects how craftsmen seek opportunities of rich patronage, and also shows why it is difficult to separate these regions into distinct stylistic categories of metalwork. Meanwhile, the discontinuation of red copper and the introduction of gold inlay show how this technique achieved ever greater luxury and affluence as it moved into the Mamluk period.

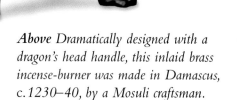

Above Dramatically designed with a dragon's head handle, this inlaid brass incense-burner was made in Damascus, c.1230–40, by a Mosuli craftsman.

of decorative frame) against densely patterned backdrops. Because the metalworker can chase lines into the inlaid silver areas, even finer detail was possible. Some of these even feature Gospel scenes, implying that not all clients in this cultural environment were Muslim.

Mosul designs are different in style to Khurasan inlaid metal pieces: the visual repertoire is wider and the metal forms they decorate are local to Mosul and the surrounding region. Craftsmen in Mosul, as in Khurasan, exploited the metal inlay technique to make their decoration more pictorial, a practice which was also fashionable in other contemporary media, such as enamelled glass and ceramics. Illustrated manuscripts that have survived from 13th-century Iraq show many parallels of composition and pictorial motifs between these paintings and the exquisite scenes composed on inlaid metal objects.

MAMLUK METALWORK IN EGYPT AND SYRIA

THE MAMLUK RULERS COMMISSIONED SPLENDID PIECES OF METALWORK, RICH WITH GOLD AND SILVER INLAY. METALWORKERS ALSO PRODUCED WARES FOR DOMESTIC AND EXPORT MARKETS.

Mamluk inlaid metalwork belongs to an art tradition that had spread across Syria and Egypt from Mosul (in northern Iraq) during the 13th century. Craftsmen used the signature *al-Mawsili* ('of Mosul') to signify their training background, even while making objects in Damascus or Cairo. Large basins, trays, bowls, pen boxes, incense-burners, ewers, candlesticks and caskets were all among the objects produced by Mamluk metalworkers.

Gold was used increasingly as an inlay, enhancing the luxury of these spectacular objects all the more. Mamluk decoration typically follows one of three key themes –

flamboyant epigraphy; figural imagery; and Chinese-style motifs reflecting contact with Mongol power in Iran – sustained into the 14th century primarily by the European export industry.

EPIGRAPHIC DECORATION

Typical *al-Mawsili* designs present a series of figural scenes describing the ruler's princely lifestyle and entourage, including royal hunts, audience scenes, grand banquets and hunting animals, as well as astrological figures of the planets and zodiac signs. While this fashion was popular in late 13th-century Mamluk metalwork, the imagery was shortly superseded by a vogue

Above This brass basin – with inlay in silver, copper and niello (a black infill substance) – dates from the early 14th century.

for large-scale inscriptions in majestic *thuluth* calligraphy, set in horizontal bands and surrounded by fine stylized patterns.

A consistent feature of early Mamluk metalwork is the heraldic blazon adopted by officers in this

Below Made in 14th-century Egypt, this brass pen box has gold and silver inlay. The exquisite decoration includes floral details and kufic *calligraphy.*

military caste system, which signalled their erstwhile positions of service. The icons of the secretary, cup-bearer, or even polo master were toted as personal badges throughout the career of an amir or sultan and were attached to their material furnishings and architectural projects. However, around 1350, these blazons were gradually replaced by the large calligraphic inscriptions naming the patron with his full titles. Both styles show how the Mamluks wanted to be associated personally with their acts of patronage, especially with charitable religious foundations, promoting themselves as pious as well as powerful.

CHINESE INFLUENCE

The presence of the Mongol dynasty, the Ilkhanids, in Iran and Iraq, bordering Mamluk territory, inspired new design ideas among Mamluk metalworkers. Despite the fact that the Mongols were political enemies of the Mamluks, elements of 'chinoiserie', or Chinese-style designs, were adapted by Mamluk artisans as a direct influence from Mongol visual culture: the lotus, peony, dragon and phoenix joined Mamluk designs across the media, including metalwork.

EUROPEAN EXPORTS

While grand epigraphy was increasingly fashionable for Mamluk-commissioned inlaid metalwork, figural imagery did continue in Mamluk production – but apparently only to satisfy a lively export market to Europe. A group of objects, many signed by the craftsman Muhammad ibn al-Zayn and datable to the mid-14th century, may belong to this category. These objects are decorated with complex figural programmes, which match Mamluk manuscript-painting style

of the same period, but not contemporary metalwork trends. The archaic design may have been retained to satisfy a Western preference for pictures over Arabic calligraphy.

Italian merchants were based chiefly in Damascus, and served a keen market for Middle Eastern luxury goods in their home cities and beyond in Western Europe. Working for export, Mamluk craftsmen left areas usually reserved for heraldic blazons blank, allowing foreign merchants to sell to prospective owners – who could add their own family crest. These blank shields are in the typical European shield shape – not the round badge of Mamluk amirs and

Above Dating from the late 13th century, this brass incense-burner with gold and silver inlay is from Damascus. It is inscribed to the powerful amir, Badr al-Din Baysari.

sultans. Certainly the evidence of European paintings is that metalwork, ceramics and textiles from the Islamic world were displayed with proud ostentation in Western European domestic contexts. An Italian pilgrim, Simone Sigoli, who visited Damascus in 1384–85, described the luxury of local metalwork:

'They also make a large quantity of basins and ewers of brass, and in truth they look like gold; and then on the said basins and ewers they put figures and leaves, and other subtle work in silver – a most beautiful thing to see...Verily if you had money in the bone of your leg, without fail you would break it off to buy of these things.'

Left This brass ewer – with gold, silver and niello inlay – is inscribed with the name and titles of al-Nasir Ahmad, who ruled briefly in 1342.

OTTOMAN METALWORK

THE OTTOMAN METALWORKERS WERE HIGHLY SKILLED CRAFTSMEN, PARTICULARLY WHEN WORKING WITH GOLD AND SILVER SET WITH PREVIOUS STONES, SUCH AS RUBIES AND GARNETS.

The collection of precious metal objects in the Topkapi Palace museum in Istanbul, although spectacular, represents only a small proportion of what the Ottoman court treasury once contained. Written sources and miniature paintings give documentary and visual evidence of all types of objects made of precious metal.

However, regular military campaigns resulted in the need to melt down silver and gold when the national coffers were empty, and re-use the metal as currency.

COURT PRODUCTION

The wave of Ottoman military conquests in the 15th century brought new lands and new peoples into the expanding empire. As a result, a wide range of metalworking traditions and techniques were introduced into the imperial workshops in Istanbul. The conquest of the Balkans, with their rich deposits of gold and silver, and craftsmen expert in the local traditions of working with precious metals, was particularly important.

Craftsmen from all over the Ottoman Empire came to Istanbul and joined the *ehl-i hiref* – an expression meaning 'communities of the talented', a title given to those working in the court ateliers. By the end of the 16th century, over 100 hundred gold and silver-smiths were listed on the palace payrolls. Other related craftsmen listed include *hakkakan* (jewellers), *kuftgeran* (gold inlayers), *kazganciyan* (coppersmiths) and *zernisani* (gold repoussé workers).

It was the custom of the Ottoman court for the princes to learn a practical skill; both Selim I

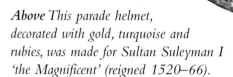

Above This parade helmet, decorated with gold, turquoise and rubies, was made for Sultan Suleyman I 'the Magnificent' (reigned 1520–66).

and Suleyman 'the Magnificent' were trained as goldsmiths and, as a result, this type of work had great social prestige. Although few signed pieces of metalwork survive from the period, one celebrated jeweller, Mehmet Usta, is known from several signed pieces.

According to an Italian merchant resident at the court of Sultan Mehmet II (reigned 1444–46, 1451–81), the sultan ate from gold plate, the viziers from silver and members of the army from base metal.

Court records list great numbers gold and silver vessels, particularly bottles and drinking cups, which were given as gifts, particularly on the important occasion of the circumcision of the young princes. Very few examples of such pieces survive today.

OTTOMAN STYLES

A number of different styles and techniques were used to produce the finest metalwork. Some of the most striking pieces are in a bejewelled style. This seems to have developed during the reign of

Left A patron of metalworkers, Suleyman I commissioned this fine pendant made of gold with pearls and emeralds for the Topkapi Palace.

Suleyman 'the Magnificent' (reigned 1520–66). Precious stones, such as rubies, emeralds or garnets were set into the surface of gold, silver and zinc objects, as well as rock crystal and jade. This most ostentatious of techniques was reserved for the most precious objects, which included Suleyman's parade helmet, decorated with rubies and turquoises, as well as his personal water flask and ceremonial sword which, in one painting, can be seen being carried by pages standing behind the Sultan.

Artisans also continued to use repoussé and other established techniques, including chasing (creating an incised design by hammering lines into the metal surface), filigree (decoration using twisted threads of gold or silver), niello (applying black inlay around engraved designs) and embossing. Unadorned pieces – such as bottles and candlesticks with bold shapes but no additional decoration – were also made. Gilded copper, or tombak, was a popular material for this plainer style of design.

FLORAL DECORATION
Floral designs transformed not only the surface of Ottoman metalwork, but also the basic form: one popular type of brass candlestick was made with the candleholder section cast in the shape of a tulip with pointed petals.

The *saz* style developed by the artist Shahquli, with its combination of serrated *saz* leaves and blossoms, was adopted by goldsmiths; a certain Mehmed the Bosnian excelled at this style and at least three signed examples of his work survive in the Topkapi Palace museum. During the 18th century, a Rococo style was adopted from Europe with the

Above These daggers with decorated sheaths date from c.1600, in the reign of Mehmet III.

emphasis on floral bouquets, garlands and fluttering ribbons.

ARMOUR
Craftsmen made all types of ceremonial armour, including helmets, swords, daggers, armour and firearms for use by sultans, princes and military leaders. The blades were inlaid with gold arabesques or calligraphy, while the hilts were often adorned with jade or precious stones. Metalworkers also made practical weapons for active warfare, including swords and

battle-axes, often decorated with jewelled scabbards, sheaths and hilts.

A superb engraved helmet made for Sultan Bayezid II has survived and is kept in the Army Museum in the Hôtel National des Invalides in Paris. Measuring about 33cm (13in) in height, the helmet is made of steel and decorated with gold wire using the technique of *kuft-gari*, in which the steel surface is roughened with a chisel and a design in gold wire is hammered into it. The inscription reads: 'Allah, I am the helmet for the head of the brave imam, the fearless Sultan, the world-Emperor, the bringer of victory to Islam, the leader blessed with Allah's support and aid, al-Malik al-Nasir Sultan Bayezid, on of Sultan Muhammad Khan, may his followers and supporters be granted greatness by Allah.'

An example of a 15th–16th-century Ottoman ceremonial dagger with a steel blade, about 20cm (8in) in length, has survived and is held in the Royal Scottish Museum, Edinburgh. It bears decoration of arabesque foliage and a calligraphic inscription inlaid in gold, from a poem by the poet Necati (d.1509). The hilt is made from grey-green jade.

Left The handle of this 16th-century golden jug, commissioned by Suleyman I, represents a dragon. The jug is encrusted with rubies and emeralds.

JEWELLERY

WORN BY BOTH MEN AND WOMEN, MUGHAL JEWELLERY WAS THE MOST OPULENT IN THE ISLAMIC WORLD. PRECIOUS STONES WERE ALSO USED IN THE ORNAMENTATION OF OTHER OBJECTS.

An Italian visitor to India in the second half of the 17th century was astonished by the conspicuous consumption and display at the Mughal court. 'In the Mughal kingdom,' he wrote, 'the nobles, and above all the king, live with such ostentation that the most sumptuous European courts cannot compare in richness and magnificence with the lustre beheld in the Indian court.'

The splendour of the court was enhanced by the custom of giving and receiving presents. When the emperor received honoured guests, he presented them with gifts, such as robes of honour, gold, silver and richly decorated swords and daggers. Sir Thomas Roe, the English ambassador at Jahangir's court, received a gold cup from the emperor, which was 'set all over with small turquoises and rubies, the cover the same set with great turquoises, rubies and emeralds…'

However, the custom also worked in reverse: to gain an audience with the emperor, it was obligatory for the visitor to present him with some precious object. 'For no man,' wrote a visiting French jeweller, 'must come into his presence empty-handed, though it be an honour dearly purchased.' Courtiers, too, were required to give expensive gifts to the emperor and to important members of the imperial household.

SUPPLYING THE DEMAND

This constant demand for jewelled objects was met by the imperial workshops, or *karkhanas*, which employed thousands of skilled craftsmen, many of them foreigners who had been attracted to India by the enormous wealth of the Mughal court. According to an account by one of Akbar's courtiers, gems could be purchased in the town markets. After a visit to Bijapur, he wrote: 'In the jewellers' shops were jewels of all sorts, wrought into a variety of articles, such as daggers, knives, mirrors, necklaces, and also in the form of birds…all studded with valuable jewels, and arranged upon shelves, rising one above the other.'

Left A naturalistic floral design is carved into this dark green, hexagonal Mughal emerald – a decoration reflecting their love of nature.

Above Emperor Shah Jahan was the most extravagant of all the Mughal emperors. He regularly wore diamonds weighing over 50 carats.

MALE JEWELLERY

All the Mughal emperors, especially Jahangir (reigned 1605–27) and Shah Jahan (reigned 1628–58), were festooned with jewels. 'For the Mughals, though his clothing be not so rich and costly, yet I believe that there is never a monarch in the whole world that is daily adorned with so many jewels as he himself,' reported an English clergyman at Jahangir's court. Akbar's jewels were all given names, while Jahangir had his arranged in such a way that he could wear a different set each day.

Pearls played an especially important role. By the time of Akbar (reigned 1556–1605), double and triple strands of pearls were symbols of nobility. Portraits of the emperors also show them wearing enamelled gold armlets, jewelled turban ornaments, pearl earrings, gold bracelets inset with diamonds and rubies, archer's rings on their thumbs and pendants with rubies and emeralds.

FEMALE JEWELLERY

The imperial ladies wore earrings, armlets, forehead ornaments, rings, bracelets, gem-studded necklaces and several ropes of pearls, which hung down to below their waists. In the harem, the concubines were similarly bedecked: according to one French visitor, they wore the sleeves of their thin dresses short so that 'they may have liberty to adorn the rest of their arm with carcanets (chains) and bracelets of gold, silver and ivory, or set with precious stones…'

OTHER BEJEWELLED ITEMS

The goldsmith's art was even applied to weapons: dagger and sword hilts, which were often made of hard stones, such as jade and rock crystal, were carved and encrusted with gold and precious stones.

Left Known as 'The Carew Spinel', this gemstone is inscribed with the names of three Mughal emperors – Jahangir, Shah Jahan and Aurangzeb.

However, the object that came to symbolize the splendour of the Mughal court was Shah Jahan's Peacock Throne. This celebrated throne, which took seven years to construct, was commissioned by the emperor at his coronation as a means of displaying the incredible wealth of jewels in the royal treasury. Contemporary accounts give conflicting descriptions, but paintings show Shah Jahan seated cross-

Above This early 18th-century Mughal miniature painting depicts a noblewoman wearing earrings and a necklace made with pearls, emeralds and red spinels.

legged on a four-legged dais, with four columns supporting a domed canopy. Above the canopy was a peacock, its raised tail studded with sapphires and other precious stones. In the centre of its breast lay a great ruby, given by Shah Abbas, the Safavid emperor, to Jahangir. Every surface of the throne was encrusted with diamonds, pearls, emeralds and rubies. In 1739, it was looted by Nadir Shah and carried off to Iran, and a decade later it was destroyed.

113

OTTOMAN COSTUME

MEMBERS OF THE OTTOMAN COURT – FROM RULER TO SLAVE –
WORE OSTENTATIOUS AND THEATRICAL CEREMONIAL CLOTHING
MADE FROM LUXURY WOVEN FABRICS.

Expensive and elaborate clothing formed a significant part of court life under the Ottomans, and conveyed important messages about the wearer. The Topkapi Palace in Istanbul houses more than 2,500 textiles, including no fewer than 1,000 kaftans.

On Friday, the Ottoman sultan went in public procession to attend noon prayers at a mosque outside the palace. On formal occasions such as this, he typically wore decorated gold and silver cloth, called *seraser* in Turkish, and a brooch with precious stones in his turban. Foreign dignitaries visiting the Ottoman court were invited to watch the procession, and were impressed by the wealth on display.

A decorative motif of 'tiger stripes' and three spots was often used in Ottoman art. The design was already centuries old by the time of the Ottoman era, and its constituent elements were reputedly based on the stripes and spots on tiger and leopard skins. It appears on a fragment of a kaftan that belonged to Sultan Mehmet 'the Conqueror' (reigned 1444–46, 1451–81) held in the Topkapi Palace Museum in Istanbul.

On some occasions, however, sultans wore plain materials. At funerals, for example, the sultans dressed in plain purple, dark blue or black kaftans of pure silk or mohair; for accession ceremonies, the new sultan wore white. Beneath the luxury of silk kaftans, they would wear more humble material – to avoid directly contravening the Quranic ban on wearing silk.

The sultan generally changed his silk robes after wearing them once, and afterward they were cared for by the wardrobe master in the treasury. After the death of a sultan his clothes were labelled and placed in the treasury; one of his kaftans, a turban, a belt and a dagger were laid on his tomb for the funeral.

Above Floral designs decorate the robes worn by Sultan Suleyman 'the Magnificent' in this portrait. He wears a jewelled brooch in his turban.

ROBES OF HONOUR

Many fine textiles and kaftans were given as 'robes of honour' by the sultan to leading officials or to visiting dignitaries. Called *khila*, these robes were of varying quality according to the degree of honour bestowed. This ancient Middle-Eastern system therefore expressed a strict and subtle social code. The robes given to the Grand vizier were usually made of gold or silver cloth and given in pairs: one lined with sable fur, one without. Religious scholars would only wear fine wool or mohair, but never silk.

A group of court tailors called *hayyatin-i hassa* were detailed to produce the *khila* robes. A fine silk kaftan with elongated ornamental

Left Courtiers gather for a reception at the court of Selim III (reigned 1789–1807). Splendid costumes added to the Ottoman court's projected image of power.

sleeves and a large pattern of leaves embroidered in gold on a silver ground, dated to c.1760, was given to and worn by an envoy of Frederick the Great of Prussia (reigned 1740–86) to the court of Ottoman Sultan Mustafa III (reigned 1757–74). It survives in good condition and is held in the Staatliche Museen zu Berlin in Germany.

STATUS AND CLOTHES

Clothes played an important role in Ottoman society, displaying the social status and allegiances of the wearer. Only courtiers and the wealthy elite wore kaftans and fine embroidered clothing, while poorer people wore more practical clothes.

In the era of Suleyman 'the Magnificent' (reigned 1520–66), clothing regulations were issued. Poorer men and women often wore *salvar* (trousers) or *potur* (breeches) with *mintan* (jackets) and *cizme* (boots). Strict rules

Right This silk robe, which belonged to Sultan Bayezid II (reigned 1481–1512), is in the collection at the Treasury of Topkapi Palace, Istanbul.

were laid down covering the clothes that state officials, members of the military and Christian and Jewish religious leaders could wear.

In a reform known as the *Tanzimet* (Reordering) Period in the mid-19th century, Western-style clothing, such as the waistcoat, necktie and high-heeled shoes, became fashionable among the wealthy; poorer people still wore traditional clothing.

FROM TURBAN TO FEZ

Headgear was highly significant in Ottoman visual culture: in the 16th–18th centuries people wore either the *sarik* (turban) or a cone-shaped headdress called *bashlyk*. The *sarik* was made out of particularly fine material. In 1826, under Sultan Mahmud II, the short cone-shaped felt hat called the fez replaced the *sarik*. Then, in 1925, after the foundation of the Republic of Turkey, Mustafa Kemal Ataturk outlawed the fez as part of a series of modernizing and secularizing reforms. As a result, more people began to wear Western-style hats, which were manufactured to meet the increased demand.

OTTOMAN SILK AND VELVET WORK

The Ottomans ran a thriving industry in silks and velvet, with production based at Bursa. Weavers used patterns based on crescents, leopard spots and tiger stripes, and a lattice enclosing flowers, such as tulips. Patterns were often in gold on a crimson ground. Weavers used silk for court kaftans and covers to be laid on the tombs of sultans and great officials; the tomb covers were embroidered with Quranic verses and invocations to Allah. A beautiful 18th-century red silk tomb cover of this kind is held in the Victoria and Albert Museum, London. Velvet was used for divan cushion covers, large hangings and saddle covers. A fine velvet saddle cloth embroidered in silver and gilt wire with flowers and foliage was given to King Gustavus Adolphus of Sweden in 1626 and is kept in the Royal Armoury, Stockholm.

Right A warrior horseman is shown wearing a wonderful silk robe in this battle scene from the Suleymanname.

PERSIAN CARPETS

UNDER THE SAFAVID DYNASTY, CARPET WEAVING WAS TRANSFORMED INTO A STATE-SPONSORED INDUSTRY, PRODUCING SPLENDID CARPETS FOR BOTH RELIGIOUS AND PALATIAL CONTEXTS.

The weaving of carpets was an ancient art form in the Islamic world, and fragments of rugs and carpets survive from Seljuk Anatolia and Mamluk Egypt. The oldest complete, dated Islamic carpets, however, are from Safavid Iran.

Many carpet designs echoed the composition of contemporary book covers, with an elongated rectangular layout in which the central area was set within borders. Figurative designs were often similar to those in book illustrations, and indeed could have been designed by the same artists, while others consisted of repeating abstract patterns.

THE ARDABIL CARPETS

One common carpet design, which gave rise to the term 'medallion carpets', featured a large central medallion, sometimes with quartered medallions placed at the four corners. Two especially large medallion carpets were made on

Above This detail of this 16th-century hunting carpet shows a horseman turning in the saddle to fight off a lion.

the order of Shah Tahmasp for the Safavid family shrine in Ardabil in 1539–40. These are known as the Ardabil carpets, and they are probably the most celebrated of all Persian carpets.

Designed as a matching pair, the carpets consist of a densely knotted wool pile on a white silk warp and weft foundation, and feature an intricate design rendered in ten deep colours. A central yellow medallion is surrounded by a circle of smaller oval shapes, and two lamps are represented as if hanging from the medallion. All are set on a dark blue ground filled with curling scrolls of lotus flowers. A quarter section of the medallion is repeated in each corner, giving the sense of a continuing pattern. The whole design is framed by a border of patterned parallel bands.

In the late 19th century, pieces from one carpet were used to repair the other, altering their sizes. The larger carpet, now in the Victoria and Albert Museum in London, measures an immense 10.5m by 5.3m (34ft 6in by 17ft 6in), and contains 33 million woollen knots. The smaller, now in the Los Angeles County Museum of Art, California, measures 7.2m by 4m (23ft 7in by 13ft 1in).

SAFAVID SILKS

French traveller Jean Baptiste Tavernier (1605–89) claimed that more people worked at silk weaving than in any other trade in Safavid Iran. Shah Abbas I (reigned 1587–1629) revived the textile industry in Iran, establishing factories across the empire in Isfahan, Kashan, Kirman, Mashhad, Yazd and elsewhere. Many silks bore figurative images, derived from contemporary manuscript painting, of courtly picnics, lovers, huntsmen, warriors leading prisoners and scenes from the works of the poets Firdawsi (c.935–c.1020) and Nizami Ganjavi (1141–1209). In England, in 1599, the Earl of Leicester gave a set of Safavid silk hangings to Queen Elizabeth I to be hung in an apartment in Hampton Court Palace.

Left This elegant 17th-century Persian silk panel shows a pair of courtiers, in perfect symmetry, at a country picnic.

Each carpet also features a text-panel of poetry at one end:

'Except for thy threshold, there is no refuge for me in all the world. Except for this door there is no resting-place for my head. The work of the slave of the portal, Maqsud Kashani. 946.'

The number refers to the year 946 in the Hijra calendar, corresponding to 1539–40CE. Maqsud Kashani may have been the designer of the carpets or the court official who organized their production on behalf of Shah Tahmasp.

FIGURATIVE SCENES

The Ardabil carpets do not feature animals or people in their design because they were made for a religious environment. Safavid carpets designed for more secular courtly locations were frequently decorated with figural motifs.

Pairs of animals were artfully depicted in combat poses, and represented natural enemies: lion against bull, snow leopard against mountain goat, and even falcons against waterbirds. Supernatural animals were also very popular:

Above The two hanging lamps on this Ardabil carpet vary in size – perhaps to correct the perspective effect when this gigantic carpet is viewed from one end.

fighting dragons, phoenixes and chilins, all borrowed from Chinese art – without their associated symbolic meanings.

Another category of Safavid carpet depicted hunting scenes. These carpets were decorated with hunters mounted on horseback pursuing their prey, often set within borders containing kings, courtiers and musicians and, sometimes, angels. A celebrated example is the carpet created by master weaver Ghiyath al-Din Jami in 1542–43, and today held in the Museo Poldi Pezzoli in Milan, Italy. The carpet is made of wool, silk and cotton, and is precisely twice as long as it is wide, measuring 3.4m by 6.8m (11ft by 22ft).

The category known as garden carpets represented cultivated flowerbeds and trees; fish and ducks in waterways and ponds; garden pavilions, terracing and fountains; and animals such as deer, peacocks,

hares and even lions and leopards. Other carpet designs showed vases and flowers.

Some of the garden and hunting carpets also featured medallions in their design. On the Ghiyath al-Din Jami hunting carpet in Milan, for example, the hunting scenes were arranged around a medallion, while in the corners of the design were cranes set amid bands of cloud.

EXPORTS

Fine carpets made excellent diplomatic gifts and were also widely exported. Under Shah Abbas I (reigned 1587–1629), a number of carpets were made in the royal workshops in Isfahan and Kashan to be given as gifts to foreign rulers, or were commissioned by patrons in Europe. Examples include a group bought by King Sigismund III Vasa of Poland in 1602, complete with the royal coat of arms, while silk carpets were given to the doges of Venice in 1603 and 1622. Exported Safavid carpets, sometimes known as 'Polonaise' carpets, were discovered in Poland in the 19th century.

INDIAN CARPETS AND TEXTILES

THE SPLENDOUR OF MUGHAL INDIAN CARPETS AND TEXTILES MAY BE SEEN IN CONTEMPORARY COURT PAINTINGS, WHICH SHOW THE LUXURY OF COURT DRESS AND FURNISHINGS.

The luxury textiles of the Mughal court included silk embroidered cottons, velvets and woven silks, as well as carpets with sophisticated designs. The earliest written evidence that knotted pile carpets were being manufactured in Mughal India appears in the *Ain-i Akbari*, the chronicles of the emperor Akbar (reined 1556–1605). The court biographer Abu'l-Fazl relates that in the 1560s, the emperor '…has caused carpets to be made of wonderful varieties and charming textures; he has appointed experienced workmen, who have produced many masterpieces… All kinds of carpet weavers have settled here, and drive a flourishing trade.'

The most valuable carpets and textiles were stored in the *farrashkhana* (private storehouse) at Fatehpur Sikri. In fact, the evidence of Mughal manuscript paintings shows that knotted pile carpets had been used in India before this time, since the early 16th century, at least. Indian carpets were also produced in other courts beyond the Mughal empire, such as the Deccani Sultanate further south.

EARLY MUGHAL CARPETS

The influence of Iranian design is an important aspect of early Mughal art across all media. Classic subjects depicted on Mughal carpets are therefore also found abundantly in the carpets of contemporary Iran: these include hunting scenes, with horsemen racing through an stylized natural environment and spearing game, as well as wild animal hunts, with lions seizing deer, and other animal combats. In spite of this similarity in design motifs, Indian carpets typically follow a different weave structure to carpets woven in Iran.

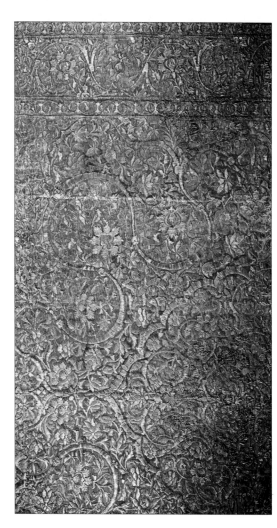

Left This red silk carpet is decorated with silver thread to create a complex floral design.

Above This carpet features a floral design organized in a tight lattice.

From the outset, European visitors to the Mughal court were greatly impressed, and took sophisticated textiles and carpets back home. Some even ordered personalized new carpets which included their family coats-of-arms in the woven pattern, such as the famous Fremlin Carpet now housed in the Victoria and Albert Museum in London. Woven in Lahore around 1640, the carpet was commissioned by William Fremlin, who served in the East India Company from 1626–44, and features his Suffolk family's crest throughout the design. Similarly, Sir Thomas Roe, the English ambassador to the court of emperor Jahangir (reigned 1605–27), recorded that he returned from India with 'a great carpet with my arms thereon'.

FLORAL DESIGNS

Many Mughal carpets with exquisite floral designs survive from the mid-17th century, often focusing on single-stem flowers with attentive detail. These reflect the wider trend for a precise

Right These woven fragments from a large court carpet feature leafy spiral scrolls which are sprouting animal heads as well as flowers.

botanical style in Mughal art during the reign of Shah Jahan (1628–58), which is found in the *pietra dura* stone inlay panels of the Taj Mahal, and in album-paintings of the same period. Plant stems and blossoms were also organized in more stylized patterns, forming spiralling scrolls or trellis grids to create delicate and complex surface designs.

Colourful printed cotton panels with all-over floral designs or bunches of flowers set within niches were hung up on palace walls and inside tents set up for the ruler's comfort and pleasure while he was out on hunting expeditions or campaigning.

CARPETS AND TEXTILES IN PAINTINGS

Manuscript illustrations reveal the important role of carpets and textiles in Mughal visual culture. Carpets were laid down not only on palace floors, but also outside in gardens, tombs and imperial tents. When Shah Jahan received important visitors in his Hall of Private Audience, every surface of the room was covered in exquisite silk carpets.

Mughal paintings show how the court was 'dressed' in this way for major diplomatic events to project the power and sophistication of the empire. Luxury textiles were distributed to courtiers in reward for loyal service, and the wearing of fine costume at court demonstrated a courtier's favourable position, as well as his wealth. Foreign textiles were also offered as diplomatic gifts to visiting ambassadors, and were received with interest.

Left Emperor Akbar Shah II sitting on a dais with his sons.

OTTOMAN CARPETS

FROM THE 15TH CENTURY ONWARD, MANY FINE CARPETS WERE PRODUCED FOR THE IMPERIAL COURT IN ISTANBUL OR FOR EXPORT TO EUROPE. PRAYER RUGS WERE ALSO MADE FOR THE FAITHFUL.

The finest Ottoman carpets were produced in Ushak, in western Anatolia. Carpets from this region, now known as Ushak carpets, were commissioned by the Ottoman court under sultans Mehmet II (reigned 1444–46, 1451–81) and Bayezid II (reigned 1481–1512). The Ottomans held a strong, central control over the artistic production of the carpets, and the designs reflected their tastes.

REDS DOMINATE

The carpets have fine designs, usually organized in a repeated series of motifs and following a strict symmetry. The colour palette was dominated by red, with design elements in green, white, yellow and blue. Some of the Ushak carpets were manufactured in a large format, up to 10m (33ft) in length.

Below This 17th-century Star Ushak rug is the only surviving complete example of a design that uses quatrefoil (four-leaved) medallions with smaller diamonds.

Ushak carpets have been divided into several groups based on design. One major group is known as the 'Star Ushaks' because these carpets bear an endlessly repeating design of an eight-pointed star alternating with a smaller lozenge. Another group is known as the 'Medallion Ushaks' because they were decorated with a medallion design. Designs such as these remained in use for long periods under the Ottomans.

EXPORTS FOR EUROPE

Many fine Ottoman carpets were exported to Europe, especially via Italy, from the 15th century onward. Members of the nobility and church authorities were frequent buyers; the rugs were prestigious possessions, and were represented by leading artists in portraits and in sacred paintings intended for churches (*see* Holbeins and Lottos, opposite). Henry VIII had extensive collections of Turkish and Egyptian carpets: by his death in 1547, there were 500 such carpets in Tudor palaces.

Above The Ottomans added floral designs to the prayer rugs they commissioned. This rug was woven from wool and cotton in c.1600.

PRAYER RUGS

Another category of carpet was the prayer rug or *saf*. These were intended for use by the Muslim faithful in mosques. They carried an image of the *mihrab* (niche) and were laid on the floor pointing toward Makkah when, during prayers, worshippers prostrated themselves in the direction of the holy city.

There were both single prayer rugs for individual use, and longer ones with several woven niches aligned either horizontally or vertically on the rug, designed to be shared by a number of worshippers at prayer. Few of these carpets have survived because they were in daily use during worship, but there are some surviving fragments of communal prayer rugs: some now held in the Museum of Islamic and Turkish Art in Istanbul are badly damaged but are still 8m (26ft) long, giving an idea of how long they once must have been. Ushak prayer rugs often used a cloud-bank border adopted from Persian designs; some represented a pendant to indicate a mosque lamp.

An Ottoman prayer rug in the collection of the Textile Museum in Washington, DC, is a good example of another common design featuring three prayer arches. It dates to the 1600s, and is very similar to rugs represented in 17th-century Dutch paintings, such as *Still Life* by Nicolaes van Gelder (1664), now in the Rijksmuseum, Amsterdam.

Above A prayer rug of c.1500, woven from wool in Cairo, provides ample evidence of the Mamluk artisans' skill that was so admired by the Ottomans.

MAMLUK INFLUENCE

After the Ottomans conquered Egypt in 1517 under Sultan Selim I (reigned 1512–20), they had access to the highly skilled carpet makers of Mamluk Cairo. The Mamluks used finer wool than their Turkish contemporaries, and made tighter knots to create even more elegant flowing designs; they sometimes also used cotton for the white areas of a design and silk for the main weave. Before the Ottoman conquest, they had typically woven carpets with kaleidoscopic designs and patterns of octagons with stars, in blues, green and wine-red colours. The Ottomans dispatched detailed designs for floral patterns featuring hyacinths, carnations and tulips from Istanbul to be followed by the Mamluk weavers.

In 1585, Sultan Murad III (reigned 1574–95) called 11 master carpet makers from Cairo to Istanbul, with a large consignment of Egyptian wool; at this point there were 16 master carpet makers in the Ottoman capital, but the demand for carpets was so high that they could not meet it. As a result of Egyptian influence, some carpets and rugs made in Turkey began to show Egyptian elements: for example, a rug from the mausoleum of Sultan Selim II (d.1574) used typically Egyptian green and cherry-red colours.

HOLBEINS AND LOTTOS

Certain designs of Ottoman carpets exported from Ushak became known as 'Holbeins' and 'Lottos', after the European artists Hans Holbein the Younger (1497/8–1543) and Lorenzo Lotto (c.1480–1556), in whose paintings the carpets were represented as luxury objects. The artists carefully copied the delicate patterns and rich colours of the carpets. Both designs appeared also in the works of other artists. The Holbein design, which featured octagons interlaced with cross-shaped elements, appeared in European art from 1451 onward; the first appearance of the similar Lotto design was in a 1516 portrait by Sebastiano del Piombo (c.1485–1547).

Right An Ottoman carpet takes pride of place in this portrait, Husband and Wife *(c.1523), by Italian artist Lorenzo Lotto.*

WHERE TO SEE ISLAMIC ART

THE ISLAMIC WORLD

Museum of Islamic Art, Doha, Qatar

This museum opened its doors in 2008. The building, inspired by Islamic architecture, was designed by the architect I.M. Pei. It houses Islamic artworks from the 7th to 19th centuries, including textiles, ceramics, manuscripts, metal, glass, ivory and precious stones. www.mia.org.qa/english

Iran Bastan Museum, Tehran

This national museum now incorporates two original museums that together cover ancient archaeology and many pre-Islamic artefacts and post-Islamic period artefacts. www.nationalmuseumofiran.ir

Islamic Arts Museum, Kuala Lumpur

This collection of more than 7,000 artefacts aims to be representative of the arts of the Islamic world. An emphasis is placed on works from India, China and South-east Asia. www.iamm.org.my

Museum of Islamic Art, Cairo

The renovated Museum of Islamic Art holds a collection of more than 100,000 objects of mainly Egyptian origin produced from the 7th to 19th centuries. www.islamicmuseum.gov.eg

L.A. Mayer Museum of Islamic Art, Jerusalem

Dedicated to the memory of Leo Arie Mayer, a professor of Islamic Art and Archaeology at the Hebrew University of Jerusalem, this museum aims to cultivate a mutual understanding between Jewish and Arab cultures. www.islamicart.co.il/default-eng.asp

Turkish and Islamic Arts Museum, Istanbul

The Ibrahim Pasha Palace is now home to a 40,000-strong collection of Islamic arts, and is particularly famed for its world-class selection of carpets. www.greatistanbul.com/ibrahim_pasa_palace.htm

Below Museum of Islamic Art, Doha.

Above Entry gate to the Topkapi Palace Museum, Istanbul.

Topkapi Palace Museum, Istanbul

Built in the 15th century and once the imperial residence of the Ottoman sultans, Topkapi Palace is now the setting for one of the foremost museums of Islamic art in the world. It holds first-rate collections of manuscript painting, ceramics, clothing and jewellery. www.topkapisarayi.gov.tr/eng

Tareq Rajab Museum, Hawelli, Kuwait

The private collection of the Rajab family, the museum has around 10,000 objects on permanent display. The collection managed to survive the Iraqi invasion of 1990, and the attached Museum of Islamic Calligraphy was opened in 2007. www.trmkt.com

EUROPE

British Museum, London

Concentrated in the John Addis Gallery, the Islamic collection includes artworks from the full range of Islamic history. The museum is actively collecting contemporary Islamic art. www.britishmuseum.org

Right London's Victoria and Albert Museum.

Victoria and Albert Museum, London

The Jameel Gallery at the V&A contains more than 400 objects out of a collection of 10,000 from across the Islamic world. The star piece of this magnificent collection is the Ardabil carpet, the oldest dated carpet in existence. www.vam.ac.uk

Chester Beatty Library, Dublin

Established by the American collector and magnate, this collection was gifted to the Irish Republic on Chester Beatty's death in 1968. The Islamic section is particularly strong in Mamluk Qurans, as well as Ottoman, Persian and Indian paintings. www.cbl.ie

Musée du Louvre, Paris

As of 2010, the objects from the Islamic Department of the Louvre can be found in an exhibition space in the Cour Visconti. The new building can display 3,000 objects. www.louvre.fr

Museum für Islamische Kunst (Museum of Islamic Art), Berlin

Islamic architectural decoration features strongly in this collection, housed in the south wing of the Pergamonmuseum. Its highlights include the façade of the Mshatta Palace, 13th-century *mihrabs* (niches to indicate the direction of prayer) from Konya and Kashan, and the Aleppo Room.
www.smb.spk-berlin.de

The David Collection, Copenhagen

Founded by Danish lawyer Ludvig David in his ancestral home, since his death in 1960 the David Collection has concentrated on acquiring Islamic artworks of outstanding quality, resulting in a superb collection of 2,500 objects. www.davidmus.dk

RUSSIA

State Hermitage Museum, St Petersburg

The Islamic art collection holds pieces from Iran, Egypt, Syria and Turkey. The collection includes more than 700 Iranian bronzes as well as Islamic textiles, ceramics, manuscript paintings, glassware and weaponry. www.hermitagemuseum.org

USA

Freer and Sackler Galleries at the Smithsonian, Washington, DC

The Freer and Sackler Galleries are one of the best places to see Islamic art in the United States. The collection of more than 2,200 objects is strong in the areas of ceramics and illustrated manuscripts. www.asia.si.edu/collections/islamicHome.htm

Metropolitan Museum of Art, New York

The Met's Islamic galleries display pieces from its prized collection of 12,000 objects, including ceramics, calligraphy and metalwork.
www.metmuseum.org/Works_of_Art/islamic_art

Los Angeles County Museum of Art

There are more than 1,700 Islamic objects in the museum, making it a significant collection of Islamic art in the country. Areas of note include Iranian pottery and tiles, and the Turkish arts of the book.
www.lacma.org/islamic_art/islamic.htm

ONLINE

Museum With No Frontiers (MWNF)

The largest transnational museum on the web, the MWNF's flagship project, Discover Islamic Art, contains Islamic art and monuments from around the Mediterranean, organized by country.
www.discoverislamicart.org

The Khalili Collection

With more than 20,000 Islamic artworks, the Khalili Collection is one of the most comprehensive private collections ever assembled. More than 30 museums worldwide have exhibited pieces from the collection and slideshows are available on the website.
www.khalili.org

GLOSSARY

ABLAQ Typically Syrian use of alternating dark and light masonry, often marble.

ARABESQUE Decorative geometric ornament based on stylized vegetal forms, such as tendrils and creepers.

ARCH A curved area in a building used to spread the weight of the structure above it to the walls, pillars or columns below; important in Islamic architecture, especially for supporting large domes.

ASHLAR Dressed stone blocks.

AZULEJO Tin-glazed ceramic tiles produced in Islamic Spain.

BAB Gate.

BAZAAR Turkish term for covered marketplace and business centre in Islamic towns and cities, also known as *souk* in Arabic.

CALLIGRAPHY The art of beautiful writing; in Islam stylized written Arabic is revered as the highest art because it gives visible form to the words of the holy Quran.

ÇAMI Congregational mosque used for Friday prayers (Turkish; called *jami* in Arabic).

CARAVANSERAI Secure and often fortified lodging for merchants and travellers, their animals and goods, usually on a trade route. Known as *han* in Turkish, and *khan* in Arabic.

CASBAH See citadel.

CHAHAR BAGH Persian-style, four-part garden layout.

CITADEL Enclosed, fortified section of a city or town, known as *casbah* (from Arabic *qasaba*) in North Africa.

CLOUD BAND Decorative motif of curling clouds in Chinese art, used throughout Islamic art from the 14th century onward.

CUERDA SECA (in English, 'dry cord') Use of lines of a greasy black substance to mark out and contain areas of glaze applied to tiles, enabling artists to contain the colours.

DRESSED STONE Building stone that has been shaped or 'finished' prior to use.

GUNBAD Tomb tower.

HAMMAM Bathhouse.

HAN See caravanserai.

HYPOSTYLE Hall with flat roof supported by columns; type of mosque in which the flat roof of the prayer hall is supported by rows of columns.

INLAYING The technique of inserting one material into another to create a decorative effect, often used in metalwork to add a precious metal, such as gold or silver, to decorate a less expensive metal body, such as bronze or brass.

IWAN Vaulted hall with one side left open, giving on to the courtyard of a mosque or *madrasa*.

JAMI Or *masjid-i-jami*; congregational mosque used for Friday prayers (Arabic; *çami* in Turkish).

KAABAH Islam's most sacred shrine, a cube-shaped building in the Masjid al-Haram (Holy Mosque) at Makkah; Muslims must face toward the *Kaabah* when praying.

KHAMSA Five in Arabic; in Persian a *khamsa* is a group of five books; in Islamic Africa a *hamsa* (sometimes *khamsa*) is a hand-shaped, good-luck symbol used in jewellery.

KHAN See caravanserai.

KHANQA A monastery for Sufis.

KITAB Book; al-Kitab or kitab Allah (Book of God) are sometimes used as terms for the Quran.

KUFIC Early Arabic script, named after city of Kufa in Iraq.

KULLIYE Complex of religious buildings centred on a mosque with other establishments, such as

Above Like other Ottoman sultans, Ahmet III (reigned 1703–10) was a great patron of the arts.

madrasa, caravanserai, hammam, kitchens and sometimes hospitals, typically built by wealthy subjects of the Ottoman sultans.

LUSTREWARE Ceramics finished with metallic glazes that produce a shining effect. Developed in Abbasid Iraq in the 9th century.

MADRASA Islamic educational establishment, often associated with a mosque, where students studied the Quran, law and sciences.

MAGHRIBI Cursive form of Arabic script; developed in western Islamic lands.

MAIDAN Open square, usually in the centre of a town or city.

MAQSURA Private area in a congregational mosque used by a ruler or governor, often lavishly decorated.

MASHHAD Shrine; tomb of martyr or Sufi saint.

MASHRABIYA Turned-wood openwork screen.

MASJID See mosque.

MIHRAB Wall niche in form of arch indicating the correct direction of prayer (toward Makkah).

MINAI An overglaze technique for decorating pottery used in Kashan Iran in the 12th–13th centuries.

MINARET Tower attached to a mosque, once used as a watchtower but now the place from which the Muslim faithful are called to prayer.

MINBAR Pulpit in mosque from which the *khutbah* prayer or sermon is pronounced.

MOSQUE Muslim place of gathering and prayer. In Arabic, *masjid* ('place of prostration').

MUEZZIN Anglicized form of the Arabic *muadhdhin*, the individual who calls faithful to prayer, traditionally from the minaret of a mosque.

MUHAQQAQ Cursive script used in calligraphy; one of the 'six hands' of calligraphy identified in the 10th century by Ibn Muqla (d.940).

MUQARNAS Small, concave stalactite vaults, often painted or tiled, used widely in Islamic architecture.

MUSALLA Enclosed area with *qibla* wall, where large numbers can gather to worship; known as *Namazgah* in Persian.

NASKH Style of Arabic script.

NASTALIQ Calligraphic script, used mainly for Persian rather than Arabic.

PISHTAQ Arched portal leading to an *iwan* at the entrance of a mosque, *madrasa* or *caravanserai* in Iran.

QASR Palace or castle.

QIBLA The direction of prayer, toward the *Kaabah* at Makkah, in which Muslims face when praying.

QUBBAH Dome or domed tomb.

QURAN The word of Allah (God), as revealed to the Prophet Muhammad in 610–32; the main source of guidance and authority for Muslims.

Right Blue tiles decorate an arched panel in the Friday Mosque in Isfahan, Iran.

RIBAT Fortified monastery, a base for *jihad*, or religious war.

RIWAQ Arcades running around the four sides of the courtyard in an Arabic-style courtyard mosque.

SAHN Courtyard of a mosque.

SHADIRWAN Fountain inside a palace room or the courtyard of a mosque.

SHAHNAMA Book of Kings. Epic Persian history written by Firdawsi between 977–1010. The text has been illustrated in various media.

SHEREFE Balcony on minaret used when issuing a call to prayer.

SURAH A chapter in the Quran (plural *suwar*).

TALAR Columned hall (Persian).

THULUTH Large and elegant cursive calligraphic script.

TIRAZ Robes given as mark of honour, embroidered with Quranic verses and the name of the donor.

TUGHRA Stylized monogram-signature incorporating the name of an Ottoman sultan.

TURBE Mausoleum.

ULAMA Islamic legal and religious scholars (Arabic, singular *alim*).

VIZIER Administrator; chief minister (Anglicized form of the Arabic *wazir*).

WAQF Pious endowment supporting a *masjid*, *madrasa* or secular institution, such as a *bimaristan* (hospital).

WIKALA Hostel for merchants and travellers within a city.

YURT Round tent used by Central Asian nomads.

ZIYADA The enclosure or courtyard between mosque precincts and outer walls.

INDEX

Below *Detail of the floral tile work in the Savar Garden, Shiraz, Iran.*

Below Detail of ornate inlay work at Emperor Akbar tomb at Sikandra, Agra, India.

Below Domed interior of a tomb in the Shah-i-Zinda necropolis, Samarkand.

ACKNOWLEDGEMENTS
The publishers have made every effort to trace the photograph copyright owners (t=top, b=bottom, l=left, r=right, c=centre). Anyone we have failed to reach is invited to contact Toucan Books, 89 Charterhouse Street, London EC1M 6HR, United Kingdom.

akg-images: 19t, 20t, 24t, 26b, 32t, 32b, 35b, 37, 44t, 54t, 55b, 64t, 65t, 66b, 67tr, 67b, 68b, 79b, 81b, 104t, 109t, 116t.
Alamy: 18t, 18b, 38b, 43tr, 54b, 56t, 80b, 88b, 89t, 89bl, 101b, 111tr, 116t, 122t, 127.
Ancient Art & Architecture Collection: 71t, 94t, 94b, 98t, 104b, 111b, 115b.
Art Directors/ArkReligion.com: 24t.
The Art Archive: 19b, 22t, 27t, 28b, 33, 34t, 35t, 40t, 41t, 41b, 44br, 47b, 55t, 60t, 63b, 66t, 73b, 78b, 80t, 85t, 86b, 91b, 97b, 98b, 99b, 102b, 105t, 106b, 108t, 108b, 109b, 110t, 110b, 114b, 115t, 117, 119b, 125.
The Bridgeman Art Library: 1, 3, 4, 5l, 16t, 17b, 22b, 23t, 23b, 28t, 29t, 29b, 30t, 30b, 34b, 38t, 39, 40b, 42t, 42b, 43tl, 45t, 45b, 46t, 46b, 47t, 48t, 48b, 49t, 49bl, 49br, 50t, 50b, 51t, 51b, 58t, 58b, 59t, 59b, 61tr, 61cl, 62t, 62b, 63t, 68t, 69t, 69b, 70t, 70b, 71b, 73t, 74b, 75, 76t, 77t, 77b, 78t, 79t, 82t, 82b, 84t, 84b, 89br, 93, 95b, 96t, 96b, 97t, 100t, 102t, 103t, 103b, 106t, 112, 113b, 114t, 116b, 118t, 119t, 120t, 121t, 121b, 124.
Corbis: 2, 5r, 6, 7, 8, 9, 10, 11, 12t, 14, 15, 21tl, 21tr, 24b, 25b, 26t, 27b, 31, 36t, 36b, 52, 53, 57t, 72t, 72b, 74t, 76b, 90b, 91t, 92, 113t, 120b, 126, 128.
Heritage-Images: 13, 56b.
Peter Sanders Photography: 21b.
Photoshot: 87b, 107t, 123.
Photolibrary: 64b, 86t, 88t, 122b.
Rex Features: 57b, 105b, 107b.
Robert Harding: 85b, 87t, 90t.
Werner Forman Archive: 16b, 17t, 60–61b, 65b, 81t, 83t, 83b, 99tr, 100b, 101t, 118b.